Accelerated Action Learning

In a knowledge-based society, people should not simply collect knowledge but should utilize and apply it to solve a problem. Action learning makes organizational members learn while solving real problems in the workplace. However, traditional action learning might not be effective for rapidly changing environments, because it is typically a process that requires substantial time. Therefore, this book provides a guideline on how to apply action learning quickly in workplaces—especially in virtual settings.

Action learning allows the organization to develop people while, at the same time, getting work done. It is an alternative to classroom-based and online learning programs. In addition, it can also be an alternative to the instructional systems design (ISD) model or the successive approximation model (SAM) as a means of developing planned instruction if used for that purpose. Action learning can be an effective tool for Web 2.0 learning. Many organizations are now using self-directed teams and other team formats for work. It makes sense to revisit planned on-the-job training and learning with an emphasis on teams. Action learning is a process involving a small group with facilitators and action-learning process managers, so it is one of the best options for team-based problem-solving.

This book provides real action learning cases. There are needs that have emerged in these post-pandemic times. There is a need to explain how action learning can be applied to various settings, issues, and challenges. Since COVID-19 occurred, many people must work in virtual or hybrid settings. This book gives trainers—who could be HR managers, operating managers, or learning and development professionals—guidelines that can be used in virtual settings to meet the new needs.

Essentially, this book is written for team facilitators, supervisors, managers, or team members who wish to plan action-oriented, problem-based, and work-related learning experiences in real time. Because many action-learning books are written for an academic audience, it is not easy to put action learning into practice. Therefore, the goal of this book is to provide guidelines on how action learning starts, what basic principles should be considered, and what tools and techniques are needed for rapid action learning. The book is intended to be a primer on how to facilitate a planned learning project in a team or workgroup.

Accelerated Action Learning

Using a Hands-on Talent Development
Strategy to Solve Problems, Innovate
Solutions, and Develop People

By

William J. Rothwell, Smita Singh (Dabholkar), and
Jihye Lee

Foreword by Michael Marquardt

Routledge
Taylor & Francis Group

A PRODUCTIVITY PRESS BOOK

First published 2024
by Routledge
605 Third Avenue, New York, NY 10158

and by Routledge
4 Park Square, Milton Park, Abingdon, Oxon, OX14 4RN

Routledge is an imprint of the Taylor & Francis Group, an informa business

ISBN: 978-1-032-39159-5 (hbk)
ISBN: 978-1-032-39158-8 (pbk)
ISBN: 978-1-003-34865-8 (ebk)

DOI: 10.4324/9781003348658

Typeset in Garamond
by Deanta Global Publishing Services, Chennai, India

William J. Rothwell dedicates this book to his wife *Marcelina*, his daughter *Candice*, his son *Froilan*, his grandsons *Aden* and *Gabriel*, and his granddaughters *Freya* and *Lina*.

Smita Singh (Dabholkar) dedicates this book to her parents, in-laws, her husband *Abhishek*, her children *Aryan* and *Shriya*, her support staff at home, and her friends.

Jihye Lee dedicates this book to her father *Ilkwon*, her mother *Eunsil*, her husband *Joseph*, all her friends and colleagues, and *God*, who has guided her on this writing journey.

Contents

Foreword

Action learning continues to grow worldwide. Thousands of organizations are now using action learning to creatively solve complex problems, to build leadership skills, to develop stronger work teams, and to change the culture of their company. Action learning has become popular because it can accomplish great short-term results while simultaneously developing powerful long-term individual, group, and organizational capabilities.

However, there are still many leaders who hesitate to introduce action learning into their organizations. Based on their own experiences in action learning or based upon what they have heard from others, these leaders have deemed that action learning will not work in their organization. Why not? For them, the action learning process of asking questions and taking time to reflect and learn takes too long. Why ask questions when statements work faster? They feel that their current group problem-solving methodology of using statements appears quicker. They prefer that decisions and actions are controlled by those with the most experience and authority.

Of course, as many of us know too well, this type of problem-solving usually ends up solving the wrong problem and/or developing inadequate and non-sustainable strategies. Group members are frustrated because their group becomes ever more dysfunctional. The capability of the group never seems to improve and obtaining great results in a supportive environment remains elusive.

The ideal solution is to have action learning programs that are both powerful and quick. And that is what this wonderful book is all about. The pages are filled with theories, strategies, and clear directives as to how great action learning programs can be accelerated.

And why do organizations want action learning to work quickly? For two major reasons: (1) since the problem is urgent, the organization needs to have strategies and actions before the problem becomes even worse and creates a bigger crisis, and (2) if too much time is taken over several months, one or more group members may leave the group (new job, new responsibility, bored with the group, etc.). When a group member leaves the group, her wisdom, experience, and energy are lost.

I first discovered action learning in 1994 when I was asked to teach an action learning course for the George Washington University Executive Leadership Program. Over the past 30 years, I had the great good fortune of being able to lead action learning programs with hundreds of organizations in every corner of the globe. Based on these experiences, I have learned that six elements are necessary for successful action learning programs: (1) an urgent problem or challenge, (2) a group of five to eight people, (3) a questioning, reflective way of working, (4) decisions during and actions after each session, (5) learning at the individual, group, and organizational level, and (6) a skilled coach or facilitator—my greatest successes with action learning have occurred when I or someone in the group is serving as an action learning facilitator or coach.

This book is a fantastic resource of powerful, clearly written strategies and tools to ensure that all six of these elements are part of every action learning program and that each of the six elements is introduced and integrated in a manner that leads to accelerated action learning. I especially like the clear picture format of the action learning process that enables facilitators to easily describe and explain how and why action learning works.

It is important that we recognize that action learning is not only a group activity but can also be an individual activity. Each of us can do action learning on an individual, daily basis. The simplest and easiest way is for us to reflect on an experience that has just happened. For example, we have just completed a phone call with a client; we then ask ourselves a couple of questions—"What went well? What could I do better the next time I converse with this client or with a similar client?" This is called "action learning after the event." We can also do action learning before an event by simply asking, "What would I like to accomplish? What are some good questions I could ask the client?" Finally, there can be action learning during the event in which I am reflecting on how well I am doing when the interactions are occurring. All these cases of individual action learning are examples of microlearning, in which we learn in real time to solve the daily problems or challenges that we face. This book describes how microlearning can be incorporated into each phase of action learning, making it responsive to dealing with the problems.

This book highlights the importance of question and reflection in action learning, describing how reflection can be built into each step of action learning and also how team facilitators, when used, can help learners to reflect as they solve problems in action learning sets. The wide array of clear strategies and instruments in this book will undoubtedly accelerate not only specific action learning programs but also the entire practice of action learning around the world. Thank you, authors, for this wonderful contribution to the growth of action learning worldwide.

Michael Marquardt
Professor Emeritus, George Washington University
Co-Founder, World Institute for Action Learning

Preface

By
William J. Rothwell, Smita Singh (Dabholkar), and Jihye Lee

Humans are learning beings. They learn all the time by finding and solving problems, watching other people, asking their friends or co-workers for help, and accessing such records of human experience as stories, books, and online information. Although many people associate learning with their educational experiences, most learning occurs outside educational settings as individuals grapple with the daily challenges they face in life and work.

Action Learning (AL) is a talent development strategy that can be used in organizations to help workers meet work challenges. AL is focused on solving problems. Although many models and approaches to AL exist, they have several elements in common:

- People usually—but not always—work in teams or groups to find, frame, or solve problems or address issues
- Equal emphasis is placed on addressing issues of importance to the organization and developing individuals and a team or group
- Learning experiences occur in or near the work setting.

Because AL is often focused on solving problems in real time, it is a powerful way to build intellectual capital, realize the promise of learning organizations, and develop individuals for the present and for the future.

AL relies on learning projects. A *learning project* is a "series of related episodes, adding up to at least seven hours. In each episode, more than half of the person's total motivation is to gain and retain fairly clear knowledge and skill" (Tough, 1979, p. 6). Tough's (1979) classic research, published in *The Adult's Learning Projects: A Fresh Approach to Theory and Practice in Adult Learning* (2nd ed.; Toronto: Ontario Institute for Studies), demonstrated that "almost everyone undertakes at least one or two major learning efforts each year, and some individuals undertake as many as 15 or 20 … It is common for a man or woman to spend 700 hours a year at learning projects" (Tough, 1979, p. 1). Projects can be powerful ways to guide learning—and develop people. They can be assigned by others or initiated by individuals or self-organizing teams.

At one time, AL was primarily associated with Executive Development and Management Development, conducted in classroom settings. It was also sometimes used to customize purchased training programs as well, so that they fit a unique national or corporate cultural context. But AL can be applied to other uses as well. More recently, it has been seen as a strategy for developing all job categories—not just executives or managers.

First, AL can be focused on finding or solving real-world problems. Teams or groups are commissioned to clarify a problem or issue, gather information about it and find possible solutions, experiment with innovative solutions, and evaluate the results of team experiments. By forming a group or team knowledgeable about an issue, the organization's decision-makers demonstrate a genuine commitment to empowering employees and giving them free rein to try out and carve out solutions to tough problems. In this sense, AL bears a resemblance to process improvement teams.

Second, AL can be applied as an alternative to traditional approaches to training design in which instructional designers shoulder most or all of the burden to answer such questions as these:

- Is it a problem or issue that can be solved by training?
- What is the gap between what people need to know or do to perform and what people know?
- Who are the targeted learners, how will the work setting influence the application of training, and how will the work that learners do influence the application of training?
- What should learners know, do, or feel upon completion of training?
- How will learners' proficiency in training be measured?
- In what sequence should topics be presented to learners?
- What methods and materials should be used to present training?
- How should training be delivered?
- How can training be tried before widespread delivery to field test it, and how can the results of a field test be used?
- How should the results of training be evaluated?

Using Action Learning teams to answer any of the questions above conforms with current trends that favor empowering learners to assess their own learning needs, find the means to meet their needs, conduct learning in real time (and in on-the-job) situations, and evaluate results.

Third, and finally, AL places equal emphasis on problem-solving and individual or group development. People learn as a byproduct of their work experience. Working on an AL team is an important source of learning about problem-solving approaches and working cohesively in teams or groups. Individuals learn from their peers as they participate on an AL team, usually helped by an *AL set advisor* (also known as a *team facilitator*).

Familiarity with AL is growing to be more important to practicing managers, HR professionals, and talent development practitioners. Developing individuals and teams increasingly occurs in work sites and away from quiet classroom settings. Managers will often take ownership of that process, either through their coaching or by creating an Action Learning process by which to encourage real-time problem-solving and learning.

This book moves beyond simply introducing Action Learning to showing how learning from work experience can be managed faster and in bite-sized microlearning, to align better with today's dynamic workplaces. The book's audience may thus include business and industry talent developers, trainers, instructional designers, supervisors, managers, executives, team leaders, team facilitators, organization development practitioners, and human resource management professionals.

The Purpose of the Book

This book serves a four-fold purpose. The first purpose is to show how Action Learning can be a fast, often virtual real-time strategy for problem-finding or problem-solving. It can be a valuable tool combined with microlearning to tackle business problems and meet business needs. The second purpose is to show how Action Learning can be applied to training design. It is intended to stimulate the thinking of instructional designers about a new way to analyze needs, design and develop training, deliver training, and evaluate results. The third purpose is to show how Action Learning can be maximized to build intellectual capital and develop human talent. The book shows how team or group work can become a means for developing people in their own right. The fourth purpose is to show that Action Learning can be accelerated and thus become a means by which to push learning into real-time work and tie effectively to microlearning.

How the Book Is Organized

This book consists of twelve chapters and three appendices.

The book opens with a **Preface,** a **Glossary of Key Terms**, and **Frequently Asked Questions (FAQs) about Accelerated Action Learning**.

Chapter 1, entitled "What is Traditional Action Learning, and How Does It Differ from Accelerated Action Learning?," opens with several case stories that demonstrate typical issues encountered by organizations. The chapter then defines Traditional Action Learning and distinguishes it from Accelerated Action Learning (AAL). The remainder of Chapter 1 describes a ten-phase Accelerated Action Learning Model (AALM), explains how AALM relates to the popular 70-20-10 rule so often used by organizations, summarizes alternative approaches to action learning, and concludes with a tool to guide accelerated action learning.

Chapter 2, entitled "Phase 1: Selecting a Business Problem, Training Challenge, Organizational Vision, or Business Goal," examines the first phase of the AALM. The chapter opens with a case story. The chapter clarifies when AALM should be used and offers four steps to select a problem, challenge, vision, or goal suitable for AALM. Additionally, the chapter reviews the role played by microlearning in the first phase, describes the roles that team leaders and team facilitators play in this phase, summarizes how individual reflection plays a part in this phase, discusses differences between virtual and hybrid applications of AALM in this phase, addresses how this phase is evaluated and explains how common mistakes in this phase may be avoided. The chapter ends with a tool for selecting issues suitable for Action Learning.

Chapter 3 is entitled "Phase 2. Forming a Small Group or Team of People Meeting Criteria." This chapter opens with a case story and reviews four steps in conducting this phase: (1) identify workers who know something about the problem, training, vision, or business goal; (2) identify workers in the organization with a need to be developed in the problem, training, vision, or business goal; (3) receive approval from the worker and the worker's immediate supervisor; and (4) agree on how to hold the worker accountable for performance on an Accelerated Action Learning team. Like all the chapters between Chapter 2 and Chapter 11, this chapter also examines what role microlearning plays in this phase, what roles are played by team leaders and team facilitators in this phase, how reflection is used in this phase, what issues should be considered for virtual and hybrid settings in this phase, how this phase can be evaluated, and how the most common mistakes made in this phase can be avoided. The chapter concludes with a tool for deciding how to deploy Accelerated Action Learning.

Chapter 4 is entitled "Phase 3. Briefing Team Members About the Accelerated Action Learning Set." The chapter opens with a case story to dramatize the importance of this phase. The chapter also describes three important steps during the team briefing: (1) gathering facts; (2) organizing the briefing; and (3) delivering the briefing but emphasizing that the team bears responsibility for gathering all relevant facts. The chapter also addresses such questions as: (1) what role does microlearning play in this phase? (2) what are the roles of team leaders and facilitators in the phase? (3) how is reflection used in this phase? (4) what should be considered for virtual and hybrid settings in this phase? (5) how can this phase be evaluated? (6) how can the most common mistakes in this phase be avoided? and (7) what tool can support this phase?

Chapter 5 focuses on "Phase 4: Establishing Measurable Goals for the Action Learning Set." Like most chapters in this book, it opens with a case story. The chapter then describes three important steps in this phase: (1) identifying the issues; (2) pinpointing key measurable goals with stakeholders; and (3) working with stakeholders to agree on measurable goals to be achieved by Action Learning. The chapter also addresses the same seven questions asked in other chapters.

Chapter 6 centers attention on "Phase 5: Encouraging Team Members to Experiment with Solutions." After the case story that opens most chapters, the chapter describes six steps in this phase: (1) asking a question or questions; (2) conducting background research; (3) constructing an hypothesis; (4) testing the hypothesis by doing an experiment; (5) analyzing the data and drawing a conclusion; and (6) sharing results. The chapter also addresses the same questions addressed in other chapters: (1) what role does microlearning play in this phase? (2) what are the roles of team leaders and team facilitators in this phase? (3) how is reflection used in this phase? (4) what should be considered for virtual and hybrid settings in this phase? (5) how can this phase be evaluated? (6) how can the most common mistakes in this phase be avoided? and (7) what tool can support this phase?

Chapter 7 focuses on "Phase 6. Placing Equal Emphasis on Business Results and Individual Development." Then, the chapter describes the five steps in this phase: (1) initiating the project, focused on business results and employee development; (2) planning the project with a dual emphasis on business results and employee development; (3) executing the project with dual emphasis on business results and employed development; (4) monitoring and controlling the project with dual emphasis on business results and employee development; and (5) closing the AAL team set with dual emphasis on business results and employee development. Like other chapters, this chapter also addresses these questions: (1) what role does microlearning play in this phase? (2) what are the roles of team leaders and team facilitators in this phase? (3) how is reflection used in this phase? (4) what should be considered for virtual and hybrid settings in this phase? (5) how can this phase be evaluated? (6) how can the most common mistakes in this phase be avoided? and (7) what tool can support this phase?

Chapter 8, entitled "Phase 7: Completing the Accelerated Action Learning Set," opens with a case story about this phase. It then addresses two important steps in this phase: (1) reaching a project limitation and (2) checking with stakeholders that limitations have been reached. Like other chapters, this chapter also addresses these questions: (1) what role does microlearning play in this phase? (2) what are the roles of team leaders and team facilitators in this phase? (3) how is reflection used in this phase? (4) what should be considered for virtual and hybrid settings in this phase? (5) how can this phase be evaluated? (6) how can the most common mistakes in this phase be avoided? and (7) what tool can support this phase?

Chapter 9 is called "Phase 8: Debriefing the Accelerated Action Learning Team Members Collectively." Like other chapters, it opens with an illustrative case story. The chapter then examines six steps in this phase: (1) determining the goals of the group briefing; (2) determining who will attend the group briefing; (3) controlling the atmosphere of the group briefing; (4) creating questions to guide the group briefing; (5) holding the group briefing; and (6) analyzing and making use of the group briefing results. As with other chapters, it concludes by addressing such questions as these: (1) what role does microlearning play in this phase? (2) what are the roles of team leaders and team facilitators in this phase? (3) how is reflection used in this phase? (4) what should be considered for virtual and hybrid settings in this phase? (5) how can this phase be evaluated? (6) how can the most common mistakes in this phase be avoided? and (7) what tool can support this phase?

Chapter 10 is "Phase 9: Debriefing the Accelerated Action Learning Team Members Individually." Like other chapters, it opens with an illustrative case story. The chapter then examines six steps in this phase: (1) determining the goals of the individual briefing; (2) determining who will attend the individual briefing; (3) controlling the atmosphere of the individual briefing; (4) creating questions to guide the individual briefing; (5) holding the individual briefing; and (6) analyzing and making use of the individual briefing results. As with other chapters between 2 and 11, it concludes by addressing such questions as these: (1) what role does microlearning play in this phase? (2) what are the roles of team leaders and team facilitators in this phase? (3) how is reflection used in this phase? (4) what should be considered for virtual and hybrid settings in this phase? (5) how can this phase be evaluated? (6) how can the most common mistakes in this phase be avoided? and (7) what tool can support this phase?

Chapter 11 is the penultimate chapter. Entitled "Phase 10: Reassigning Accelerated Action Learning Team Members Based on Their Individual Development Needs," the chapter is like others because it opens with a case story to dramatize this phase. The chapter examines four key steps in this phase: (1) brainstorming important future issues facing the organization; (2) prioritizing the important future issues; (3) encouraging stakeholders to pinpoint and prioritize future issues suitable for Action Learning; and (4) identifying situations in which individuals could benefit from future cross-functional and/or cross-cultural exposure on a team. As with other chapters between Chapter 2 and Chapter 11, it concludes by addressing such questions as these: (1) what role does microlearning play in this phase? (2) what are the roles of team leaders and team facilitators in this phase? (3) how is reflection used in this phase? (4) what should be considered for virtual and hybrid settings in this phase? (5) how can this phase be evaluated? (6) how can the most common mistakes in this phase be avoided? and (7) what tool can support this phase?

Chapter 12 is the last chapter. It is entitled "Reflections on Accelerated Action Learning (AAL)." The chapter presents many topics about Accelerated Action Learning. There is a case story that brings together all the phases, showing how they work together. The chapter also covers such topics as

- Accelerating the learning process in the Action Learning program
- Making Accelerated Action Learning Teams self-organizing
- Accelerated Action Learning (AAL) and Talent deployment
- Identifying and overcoming barriers to Accelerated Action Learning
- Two approaches to experimentation in Accelerated Action Learning:

The analytical approach and the creative approach

- Common mistakes or problems in AAL teams
- How can an Action Learning team experiment with solutions?
- Kolb's learning cycle and Accelerated Action Learning

The book concludes with five Appendices. **Appendix I** is an assessment tool to help select or develop prospective or current Accelerated Action Learning team facilitators. **Appendix II** provides the 2022 results of a small-scale survey about Action Learning in India. **Appendix III** provides excerpts from interviews conducted with Action Learning practitioners in the United Kingdom and India. **Appendix IV** is a tabletop role-play simulation that can allow people to experience an Accelerated Action Learning set. **Appendix V** provides selected resources to take you further in your study of Action Learning. The book ends with thumbnail sketches of the three co-authors.

Acknowledgments

The editors appreciate all those who contributed to this project.

William J. Rothwell wants to express his special thanks to Smita and Jenny. They put the project plan together, conducted research to support the book, and were mindful of deadlines and publisher requirements while also shouldering the responsibilities of writing their chapters. He would also like to thank Farhan Sadique for his help with this book.

Smita Singh (Dabholkar) is grateful to Dr. William Rothwell for providing the opportunity to collaborate with him. She is happy to have Dr. Jenny as her co-author. She is appreciative of Pratyush Singh, her student at IMT Nagpur, and her associate, Ms. Apurva Kulkarni, for all their support in writing chapters and conducting research. She is also grateful to all the contributors from Action Learning Associates UK, especially Ruth Cook, for going the extra mile and connecting her peers with the authors. Thanks are due to Mr. Santosh Kher, Mr. Abhishek Kumar, Dr. Mukul Joshi, Mr. Ronak Moondra, Ms. Bhargavi Upadhyaya, and Mr. Shalabh Mittal for sharing their experiences with action learning. She is indebted to the support extended by the various organizations, which have contributed their inputs by filling out the survey questionnaire included in the book.

Jihye Lee wants to express her gratitude to Dr. Rothwell and Smita. Finding time to write this book while balancing life at work was nearly impossible, but the contribution and endless support of Dr. Rothwell and Smita made it possible to finish this book. She wants to give special thanks to her family, friends, and colleagues who inspired and encouraged her throughout this process. She also gives her humble respect to all writers working on their books at this moment as well. Finally, she is grateful to God for allowing her to share knowledge through this book with others.

William J. Rothwell
State College, Pennsylvania USA
July 2023

Smita Singh (Dabholkar)
Nagpur, MH, India
July 2023

Jihye Lee
Alexandria, Virginia USA
July 2023

About the Authors

William J. Rothwell, PhD, DBA, SPHR, SHRM-SCP, RODC, CPTD Fellow is a Distinguished Professor in the Workforce Education and Development program in the Department of Learning and Performance Systems, College of Education, on the University Park campus of The Pennsylvania State University. He has authored, coauthored, edited, or coedited 158 books since 1987. In 2022 he earned Penn State University's Global Lifetime Achievement Award, the university's highest award for doing international work that exerts a positive global influence for the university, and was also honored with the Organization Development Network's Lifetime Achievement Award. His recent books since 2017 include *Successful Supervisory Leadership: Exerting Positive Influence While Leading People* (Routledge, 2023), *Transformational Coaching* (Routledge, 2023), *Succession Planning for Small and Family Businesses* (Routledge, 2022), *High-Performance Coaching for Managers* (Routledge, 2022); *Rethinking Diversity, Equity, and Inclusion* (Routledge, 2022), *Organization Development (OD) Interventions: Executing Effective Organizational Change* (Routledge, 2021), *Virtual Coaching to Improve Group Relationships: Process Consultation Reimagined* (Routledge, 2021), *The Essential HR Guide for Small Business and Start Ups* (Society for Human Resource Management, 2020), *Increasing Learning and Development's Impact Through Accreditation* (Palgrave, 2020), *Adult Learning Basics*, 2nd ed. (Association for Talent Development Press, 2020); *Workforce Development: Guidelines for Community College Professionals*, 2nd ed. (Rowman-Littlefield, 2020), *Human Performance Improvement: Building Practitioner Performance,* 3rd ed. (Routledge, 2018), *Innovation Leadership* (Routledge, 2018), *Evaluating Organization Development: How to Ensure and Sustain the Successful Transformation* (CRC Press, 2017), *Marketing Organization Development Consulting: A How-To*

Guide for OD Consultants (CRC Press, 2017), and *Assessment and Diagnosis for Organization Development: Powerful Tools and Perspectives for the OD practitioner* (CRC Press, 2017).

Smita Singh (Dabholkar) earned her PhD in Psychology. She is an Associate Professor with the Institute of Management Technology Nagpur (MH, India). She has been teaching, training, and providing consultancy services for close to two decades in Organization Diagnosis and Behavioral Interventions. She is a certified assessor and trainer of MBTI by CPP and Emotional Intelligence by Six Seconds Global Emotional Intelligence Network. She has completed the Certificate Course for Women Directors by The Institute of Company Secretaries of India. She regularly trains senior executives and top management on leadership.

She has written two books. Her latest book is *Emotional Intelligence*, published by Cengage. She actively engages with industry associations and writes regularly in various trade journals. She serves on the selection panel of Public Sector organizations as a psychologist. She has been a Group Study exchange member in Sweden, a program sponsored by Rotary Foundation in 2008. She is a mother of two.

Jihye Lee earned her PhD in Workforce Education and Development with an emphasis on Human Resources and Development and Organization Development (HRD/OD) from The Pennsylvania State University. She is a Head of the Korea Market and a Global Program Specialist at the Association for Talent Development (ATD). Her research interest focuses on workplace learning. She has participated in many projects related to job analysis, competency modeling, training/education program development, and organizational diagnosis. She has managed global research projects such as *AI in Learning and Talent Development* and *Sales Enablement Research* as a research project manager. She leads global webinar series and creates global content for talent development professionals around the world.

Advance Organizer

By
William J. Rothwell

Complete the following Organizer before you read the book. Use it as a diagnostic tool to help you assess what you most want to know about Action Learning—and where you can find that information in this book *fast*.

The Organizer

Directions

Read each item in the Organizer below. Spend about 10 minutes on the Organizer. Be honest! Think of Action Learning as you would like it to be. Then indicate whether you would like to learn more about Action Learning efforts. For each item in the center column, indicate with a *Y* (for Yes), *N/A* (for Not Applicable), or *N* (for No) in the left-hand column whether you would like to develop yourself more on this topic. When you finish, score and interpret the results using the instructions appearing at the end of the Organizer. Then, be prepared to share your responses with others to help you think about what you most want to learn about Action Learning as a talent development strategy and technique. To learn more about one item below, refer to the number in the right-hand column to find the chapter in which the subject is discussed.

The Questions

Circle your response for each topic in the item below:	I would like to develop myself to:	Chapter in the book in which the item is covered:
Y N/A N	1. Answer this question: *What is Accelerated Action Learning and how does it differ from traditional Action Learning approaches?*	1
Y N/A N	2. Select a business problem, training challenge, organizational vision, or business goal for Accelerated Action Learning	2
Y N/A N	3. Form a small group or team of people (of about six to seven people) meeting the criteria for participation in Accelerated Action Learning	3
Y N/A N	4. Brief the team members about the Accelerated Action Learning set	4
Y N/A N	5. Establish measurable goals for the Accelerated Action Learning set	5
Y N/A N	6. Encourage team members to experiment with solutions	6
Y N/A N	7. Place equal emphasis on business results and individual development	7
Y N/A N	8. Complete the Accelerated Action Learning set	8
Y N/A N	9. Debrief the Accelerated Action Learning team members collectively	9
Y N/A N	10. Debrief the Accelerated Action Learning team members individually	10
Y N/A N	11. Reassign Action Learning team members based on their individual development needs	11
Y N/A N	12. Review important topics about Accelerated Action Learning	12
Y N/A N	13. Answer frequently asked questions (FAQs) about Accelerated Action Learning	Appendix I
Y N/A N	14. Use an assessment to pinpoint development needs on Accelerated Action Learning	Appendix II

Y N/A N	15. Experience a hands-on simulation of Accelerated Action Learning (sometimes called a "set")	Appendix III
Y N/A N	16. Find and review additional materials on Accelerated Action Learning	Appendix IV
____ **Total**		

Scoring and Interpreting the Organizer

Give yourself 1 point for each *Y* and a 0 for each *N or N/A* listed above. Total the points from the *Y* column and place the sum in the line opposite to the word **TOTAL** above. Then interpret your score:

Score	
14–16 Points	Congratulations! This book is just what you need. Read about the issue(s) you marked *Y*.
12–13 Points	You have great skills in Action Learning, but you also have areas where you could develop professionally. Read those chapters marked *Y*.
10–11 Points	You have a grasp of Action Learning, but you could still benefit from reading this book to build skills in selected areas.
0–9 Points	You believe you need little development or skill-building about Action Learning.

Glossary of Key Terms

Self-organizing teams: Self-organizing teams are autonomous groups that work together autonomously inside an organisation managing their own duties and making choices as a group, which promotes flexibility and cooperation.

Microlearning: Microlearning is the process of providing brief, focused educational materials in digital formats so that one can quickly pick up particular knowledge and skills through short courses or hands-on activities.

Rapid prototyping: Rapid prototyping is a development methodology that involves the creation of simpler product versions quickly in order to facilitate rapid iteration, feedback gathering, and improvement prior to the production of the final product.

70-20 -10 rule: The 70-20-10 rule emphasises the value of social and experiential learning by stating that people learn 70% of what they learn on the job, 20% from interactions with others, and 10% via formal schooling.

Focus group discussion: Focus group discussions are a type of qualitative research technique in which a small, varied group is led by a moderator in a discussion on particular subjects, yielding in-depth opinions and insights.

Emotional intelligence: Emotional intelligence is a critical component of leadership, decision-making, and interpersonal interactions. It entails the ability to successfully identify, control, and understand one's own emotions as well as those of others.

Appreciative inquiry: Identifying an organization's assets and strong points, encouraging creativity and teamwork by posing constructive questions, and building on past accomplishments are the main goals of appreciative inquiry.

Imposter syndrome: Imposter syndrome is a psychological pattern that causes people to feel inadequate and self-conscious despite their obvious achievement. It is characterised by people doubting their successes and fearing being exposed as frauds.

Stress management: Stress management is the application of coping mechanisms and other tactics to manage and lower stress levels in order to enhance both physical and mental well-being in a variety of spheres of life.

Forming stage: The Forming Stage is the first stage of team development, during which members establish goals, get to know one another, and decide on roles and responsibilities.

Storming: Storming is a stage of team growth characterised by disputes and arguments as participants voice their ideas and compete for power and influence.

Norming: The phase of team growth during which members settle disputes, create norms, and become closer to one another, resulting in improved cooperation and understanding.

Performing: The phase of team growth when members work together, efficiently, and synergistically to attain goals and perform at their best.

Turnover: The pace at which workers depart from a company and are replaced by new hires is known as turnover, and it frequently serves as a gauge of the stability and degree of satisfaction that exist there.

Design thinking: Design thinking is a method of problem-solving that prioritises empathy, creativity, and iterative prototyping in order to produce original answers to difficult problems.

Responsibility charting: In order to ensure efficient task management and accountability, responsibility charts are a useful tool for outlining roles and duties within a project or organisation.

Flash organizations: Flash organisations are short-term, project-based collaborations made possible by digital platforms and agile methodology. They bring together disparate teams fast to work on particular tasks.

Action learning set: A small-group learning strategy that promotes group problem-solving and skill development by having participants work together to address actual workplace issues.

Job rotations: An organisational practise that involves staff members switching between positions, divisions, or projects in order to foster a wide skill set and a more comprehensive grasp of the company.

Red herrings: Red herrings are deceptive clues or side interests that draw attention away from the actual issue or problem being addressed. They are frequently seen in situations involving decision-making or problem-solving.

Warm fuzzies: Feelings of optimism, support, or encouragement offered to people, creating a good environment and boosting self-esteem and general well-being.

Halo effect: The halo effect is a type of cognitive bias in which an individual's general perception of another person shapes their perception and interpretation of that person's actions, resulting in biassed conclusions.

Horn effect: Cognitive bias in which an individual's general unfavourable opinion shapes how particular characteristics or behaviours are seen, resulting in unwarranted negative conclusions.

Central tendency error: Central tendency mistake is a bias in performance reviews when assessors have a tendency to give all employees an average rating rather than an extreme one, which results in assessments that are less accurate and less distinguished.

Vox populi error: The fallacious assumption that a widely held opinion or belief is true, frequently ignoring opposing viewpoints and possible biases in the general public's opinion.

Kolb's learning cycle: This theory emphasises the value of real-world, experiential learning by suggesting that learning happens through a cycle of concrete experience, reflective observation, abstract conceptualization, and active exploration.

Experiential learning theory: A method of teaching that emphasises the value of firsthand experience and active participation in the process of learning, whereby students gain and apply knowledge via practical application and introspection.

Frequently Asked Questions (FAQs) About Accelerated Action Learning

Directions: Use this FAQ to build awareness of Accelerated Action Learning and to brief executives, managers, supervisors, and participants on an Accelerated Action Learning team about it.

1. What is *Action Learning?*

Action learning is a real-time learning experience that occurs on the job and with the dual—and equally important—purposes of (1) addressing a business need and (2) developing individuals by exposing them to important, challenging, and useful learning experiences.

2. How is *Accelerated Action Learning* (AAL) different from traditional *Action Learning* (AL)?

Accelerated Action Learning (AAL) should be faster than traditional *Action Learning (AL)*. It can occur in an employee huddle, comparable to a football huddle, in which workers assemble in real time to solve an immediate problem or issue facing a customer, another team, or the team facing the problem. An AAL is used in a way comparable to *rapid prototyping*, in which an idea is tried out quickly with the expectation that a quick answer will probably fail during implementation. The idea is to use trial-and-error methods quickly and learn from each failure to identify an effective solution faster.

AAL can use *microlearning* or *microtraining*, defined as learning events that can occur quickly and in a focused way to address an immediate problem.

3. Why should Accelerated Action Learning be used?

Accelerated Action Learning is used during work time to build employee knowledge, skills, and abilities.

Since Accelerated Action Learning often occurs in cross-functional teams, it also helps to build awareness among participants about other parts of the organization without rotating them physically to those other parts.

4. How can Accelerated Action Learning be used?

Accelerated Action Learning can solve work-related problems OR can design, deliver, and evaluate training.

5. What is the purpose of an Accelerated Action Learning team?

An Accelerated Action Learning team is assembled to (among other reasons):

■ Identify a problem
■ Troubleshoot or solve a problem
■ Discover a new opportunity
■ Reframe or creatively redefine a problem or issue
■ Establish a goal
■ Plan and introduce a new program
■ Create a vision of the future or an ideal state
■ Prepare a proposal to identify or solve a problem
■ Develop an action plan to implement a change in a group or the organization
■ Implement an action plan
■ Evaluate the results of an effort
■ Combine two or more of the activities above.

6. How are the participants chosen for an Accelerated Action Learning team?

Workers are chosen to participate in an Accelerated Action Learning experience based on their ability to address the issue confronting the organization and their needs to develop by experiencing specific problems, grappling with specific business challenges, or working with others possessing unique skill sets.

7. **When should Accelerated Action Learning be used?**

Accelerated Action Learning is appropriate when there is equal value to solving business problems and developing people for the future. It is especially useful when the talents of many organizational functions, groups, or processes should be brought together. Of course, AAL should also be used in a bid to develop people quickly to deal with crisis situations and emergent problems.

8. **When should Accelerated Action Learning *not* be used?**

Accelerated Action Learning should not be used when:

■ The issue or need to be addressed is simple and straightforward
■ The issue or need is pressing, and delay is impossible—as is the case during emergencies, crises, or catastrophes
■ No expertise exists in the organization to tackle the problem
■ Management does not value the opinions of workers
■ Management does not see merit in developing workers for the future.

9. **Where should Accelerated Action Learning be used?**

Accelerated Action Learning may be used in any geographical location. If an Accelerated Action Learning team is geographically scattered, however, maximum benefit will not be obtained because interpersonal interaction is important to the success of an Accelerated Action Learning experience.

It is possible to use Accelerated Action Learning in virtual settings or in hybrid environments in which workers are in the same geographical location, and others are working from home, either in the same national culture or in other, perhaps international, locations.

10. **How should Accelerated Action Learning be used?**

Although different models of AL have been proposed and used, you might think of it as a process in ten phases:

■ *Phase 1*: Select a business problem, training challenge, organizational vision, or business goal
■ *Phase 2*: Form a small group or team of people (of about five to seven people)

- *Phase 3*: Brief the team members on (1) the issue described in Phase 1 above and (2) any limitations established on the resources (time, money, staff, solution parameters) for the project
- *Phase 4*: Establish measurable goals for the Action Learning set
- *Phase 5*: Encourage team members to experiment with solutions
- *Phase 6*: Place equal emphasis on business results and individual development
- *Phase 7*: Complete the Action Learning set
- *Phase 8*: Debrief the Action Learning team members collectively
- *Phase 9*: Debrief the Action Learning team members individually
- *Phase 10*: Reassign Action Learning team members based on their individual development needs.

11. **How much does it cost to use Accelerated Action Learning, and how does that compare to its benefits?**

The cost of an Accelerated Action Learning project depends upon what the team members have been asked to examine. Its benefits, similarly, depend on the value of solving a problem for the organization. Determining the return on investment (ROI) thus hinges on identifying the costs of the problems and the financial value of the solutions.

12. **How long should an Accelerated Action Learning Team operate?**

Accelerated Action Learning teams can operate for any period. Workers may be seconded from their jobs full-time to work on a team or else may be tasked to work on an AAL team part-time while performing their full-time jobs.

13. **Who establishes and organizes an Accelerated Action Learning team?**

Management usually selects the members of an Accelerated Action Learning team. However, it is possible to use other approaches for selecting team members. For example, populating a team may be done competitively, where individuals "apply" to a special committee established to review which individuals to select for an AAL team based on how it will benefit the individuals selected.

14. **What are the different perspectives/ focus/agendas AAL teams can have?**

Accelerated Action Learning teams may address an issue of importance to the organization.

For instance, AAL teams may be chartered to focus on improving customer service, increasing product quality, or formulating organizational strategy. AAL teams may also design, deliver, and/or evaluate training.

Chapter 1

What is Traditional Action Learning, and How Does It Differ from Accelerated Action Learning?

Opening Case Stories

How does your organization solve problems and develop individuals, teams, or groups? Read the following case stories and think how your organization would manage each situation.

Case Story One

The company's CEO has announced that the company is facing massive attrition due to a recent acquisition. An internal company task force will soon be commissioned to identify ways to retain employees.

Case Story Two

Due to the sudden rise in COVID-19 cases, the Pharma company's CEO wants to increase its production capacity. The company's strategic planning committee forms a subcommittee to achieve that goal.

DOI: 10.4324/9781003348658-1

Case Story Three

Many women and a few male employees have left organizations during the pandemic, citing the need for childcare or eldercare. The company's CEO commissions a team to address this issue.

Case Story Four

A global corporation is attempting to build a management development program to ease the transition of expatriates from one nation and culture to another. The company's instructional designers are tasked to spearhead the effort and complete this program for employees across continents.

Case Story Five

The company has expanded its Enterprise Resource Planning (ERP) System to encompass all functions. A task force with a data consultant has been appointed to develop the working information system before the upcoming stakeholder meeting.

Case Story Six

The company CEO of a sports nongovernmental organization (NGO) has announced that the organization has funds left in the budget for the next six months. S/he has formed a team of individuals to identify potential sponsors and secure sponsorship.

Case Story Seven

In a logistics organization, a shipment is missing. It must be delivered urgently. This problem of a mysteriously missing shipment has happened for the third time in the last two months and therefore this problem needs to be solved to avoid repeat occurrences. An employee group assembles on their own to address this problem while learning from each other. They do not wait for managers to tell them to do that.

All the case stories above are typical examples of challenging situations that need to be addressed immediately. In the seventh case story, the reader should note that the employees came together independently without waiting for the management to form a team. The employees formed a team of their own. Such teams are called *self-organizing teams*. This is an important feature of accelerated action learning (AAL).

To understand what AAL is, first, let us have a look at traditional action learning (AL).

What is Traditional Action Learning, and How Does It Differ from Accelerated Action Learning?

This part of the chapter will define traditional action learning and show how it differs from accelerated action learning (AAL).

Defining Traditional Action Learning

Action learning (AL) is traditionally understood to be a real-time learning experience designed to meet two equally important purposes: to meet an organizational need and develop individuals or groups. As Dotlich and Noel (1998, p. 14) observe:

> Action Learning is magical, at least in the sense that it kills two birds with one stone. The process helps organizations respond to major business problems and opportunities while developing key people to lead organizations in the desired strategic directions.

Many definitions of AL have been offered. According to one such purpose, offered by Dean (1998, p. 3), AL

> is a voluntary, participant-centered, evolutionary process to solve real, systemic, and so-far-up-till-now-unresolved organizational work-cum-learning in the workplace as it applies the principle of democratic values and team learning in an environment of trust and authenticity.

AL founder Reg Revans does not define action learning.

Many action learning experiences occur in team situations. A group of professionals gather to:

■ Identify the root cause(s) of problems
■ Solve problems

- Create objectives
- Work toward achieving objectives
- Identify a common future vision
- Attempt to formulate a common future vision.

As the above case stories illustrate, organizations experience many time-bound challenges. Among them, organizations must:

- Discover business possibilities to maintain competitive advantage
- Explain or frame organizational issues
- Determine the root causes of issues
- Resolve issues
- Set objectives
- Work toward achieving objectives
- Create a shared outlook of the future
- Co-create a shared vision of the future among employees and stakeholders.

There is thus an explicit time constraint. A common thread in the above-mentioned case stories addresses "the speed of learning and finishing it in a stipulated time." Traditional action learning may take longer and not yield desired outcomes as quickly as desired or as quickly as necessity demands. In each case story, the organization is experiencing a *need for accelerated learning* due to business necessity.

The scope and nature of the learning needs described in the case stories may differ, but each is a learning need. Each could lend itself to a faster form of action learning. Exhibit 1.1 reviews each case story, showing how each would be addressed using the traditional action learning method and how each could be solved using an AAL approach.

Defining Accelerated Action Learning (AAL)

AAL is not about speeding up the process for its own sake; rather, it is a real-time learning experience that can be carried out in hybrid, onsite, or online modes with a team of people with three equally essential purposes in mind: meeting an organizational need; developing individuals or groups; and achieving the objectives at a faster pace with the help of enablers like microlearning and an emphasis on individual reflection.

The Accelerated Action Learning Model (AALM)

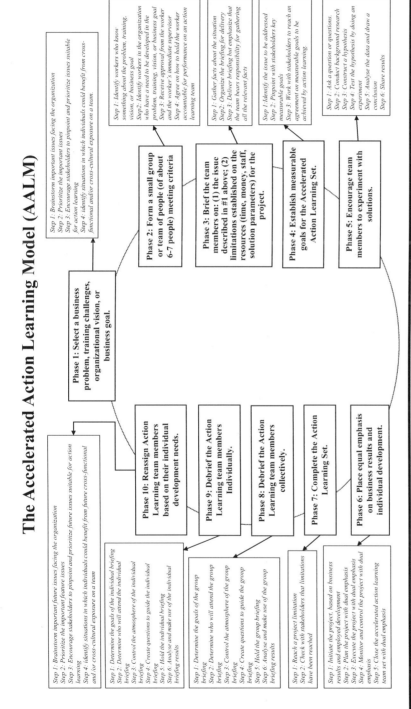

Exhibit 1.1   The Accelerated Action Learning Model (AALM)

Rapid prototyping, in which there is an emphasis on the speed of the actions taken and the feedback generated on those actions to create a scope for improvisation and modification, is a basis for AAL too (Noorani, 2008). In rapid prototyping, a rough version of a product is devised and/or launched. It is assumed that the initial prototype will not be successful but that repeated efforts at trial and error will lead to useful learning. Each revision in rapid prototyping creates a window to revisit and improve quickly, allowing one to assess a product's functionality and design. The same logic may be applied to other efforts: the launch of new services; appeal to new markets; and modifications of existing products or services to appeal to markets that are yet untapped.

Those chosen to be a part of the AAL experience have unique abilities—such as an ability to address the issue faced by the organization and the need to develop themselves by experiencing specific problems, dealing with business challenges, or working with other individuals possessing noteworthy skills. Individual skill-building occurs through problem-solving experiences.

Due to the changing nature of work in the current volatile, uncertain, complex, and ambiguous (VUCA) world, achieving results at an accelerated pace is a major challenge. There is a growing need for faster learning to cope with rapidly changing events in organizations and in the business environment. Performing at an accelerated speed is becoming a necessity to keep pace with the dynamism of business conditions today. For this reason, accelerated action learning often makes use of microlearning at every step. Gabrielli et al. (2005) note,

> Microlearning is based on the idea of developing small chunks of learning content and flexible technologies that can enable learners to access them more easily in specific moments and conditions of the day, for example, during time breaks or while on the move.

How Can Action Learning Be Accelerated?

How can action learning be accelerated? Why should it be accelerated? What are some challenges of accelerating action learning? This section addresses these critical questions.

To accelerate action learning, it is necessary to review each step of the traditional Action Learning Model (ALM) and take each step faster and more effectively to make it Accelerated Action Learning (AAL). The model guiding the chapters follows this chapter in the book (Exhibit 1.1).

What Are the Key Phases in the Accelerated Action Learning Model (AALM)?

Consider a model to guide AAL. It has ten phases. They are introduced below. Each phase is explained in detail, with the steps involved in it, in the following chapters of this book.

Phase 1: *Select a Business Problem, Training Challenge, Organizational Vision, or Business Goal*

In traditional action learning, the learning project begins with identifying a business problem, a training challenge, an organizational vision, or a business goal. An organizational leader identifies an issue an action learning team needs to address.

In Accelerated Action Learning, organizational employees are trained to recognize business problems, identify training challenges, formulate an organizational vision, or pinpoint business goals. The workers note issues needing attention without waiting for a leader to point them out. When workers take the initiative, problems are identified faster, training challenges are noticed quicker, organizational visions are formulated faster, and business goals are realized sooner.

More intrapreneurship is needed in organizations. To achieve that, work is needed to train people to think like entrepreneurs and to have the tools to act energetically and independently on their thoughts. For this new approach to work, leaders must train workers to spot problems, challenges, and opportunities, and leaders must be willing to give employees the freedom to take the initiative as they spot problems that need to be solved.

A listening framework needs to be built for employees to spot problems at the organizational level, too. It needs to have multiple listening locations and spaces for employees of the organization to gather feedback from as many stakeholders as possible. It also needs to do this regularly with missionary zeal. There should be multiple ways these data can be collected, and these aspects need to be discussed regularly with employees on as many occasions as possible. This is one way in which a listening culture could be instilled in an organization and consistency in doing this may lead to institutionalizing or creating an in-built listening framework. This way, employees can identify problems at their nascent stage.

In Taj Hotel (The Taj Mahal Palace is a heritage, five-star, luxury hotel in the Colaba area of Mumbai, Maharashtra, India), the interns are given two questions to work on: what did they see? and what did they learn? Every week when they share their observations and learnings, it becomes a repository of diagnosis, and benefits the organization in multiple ways, says Mr. H N Srinivas, former Vice President of Taj Group of Hotels, Palaces, and Resorts.

Phase 2: Form a Small Group or Team of People (of About Six to Seven People)

In traditional action learning, managers form a small group or team to address the problem, challenge, vision, or goal identified in Phase 1. They rely on two criteria to form a group: (1) each member must possess skills that seem logically related to the skills needed to solve the problem, meet the challenge, formulate the vision, or achieve the goal; and (2) each member must have a development need to learn from others on the team.

In accelerated action learning, organizational workers do not wait for managers to put them on a team. Instead, they create their teams—so-called "self-organizing teams"—to address the needs that team members identify on their own. Self-forming teams scramble to assemble faster than those that require management action to form.

Since many people are used to their supervisors telling them what to do, the organization's leaders must create a corporate culture in which people are encouraged to self-form teams that are empowered to attack problems or address other issues.

Phase 3: Brief the Team Members on (1) The Issue Described in Phase 1 Above; and (2) The Limitations Established on the Resources (Time, Money, Staff, Solution Parameters) for the Project

In traditional action learning, a manager forms an action learning team and briefs the team on the issue the team needs to address. The manager will brief the team on what he or she knows about the problem—such as whom it affects, what it is, when it began, where (what locations) in the business the problem exists, what causes the problem (why it exists), how the organization has so far tried to solve the problem, and what results stemmed from corrective actions.

In accelerated action learning, the action learning team does not wait for a manager's briefing. Instead, they research the problem or issue and gather relevant information. They self-form a team and may appoint a subgroup to gather more information about the problem. They volunteer to act.

Phase 4: Establish Measurable Goals for the Action Learning Set

In traditional action learning, a manager works with an action learning team to establish measurable goals for the action learning project. That typically involves setting parameters to govern the action learning set—such as how to define success, when to disband the team, how much authority the team must possess to hire expert help or draw on company resources, and so forth in their efforts to solve a problem, meet a training challenge, formulate a vision, or achieve a business goal. The action learning set (the learning project) is established in a way consistent with measurable goals.

Corrective action, learning, and performing at speed are prized as central corporate values, and actions reflect that bias for those goals. In accelerated action learning, the action learning team does not wait for a manager to kick-start initiatives; instead, a team self-forms and acts. Managerial approval is sought only as needed. That allows faster action not stymied by bureaucratic red tape.

Phase 5: Encourage Team Members to Experiment with Solutions

In traditional action learning, team members can experiment with solutions to solve business problems, meet training challenges, formulate visions, and/or pursue worthwhile business goals.

In accelerated action learning, team members remain free to experiment. As they do so, they rely on real-time microlearning events to learn more to solve problems, prepare training, envision new directions, or achieve business goals. Experiments are conducted faster in keeping with the philosophy of rapid prototyping. As traditionally applied, this method involves creating and testing three-dimensional prototypes of a product or feature to optimize qualities such as shape, size, and overall usefulness. However, rapid prototyping logic can create experiments to try out new ideas, or novel approaches to solve problems, meet training challenges, formulate visions, or establish and achieve worthwhile business goals.

Phase 6: *Place Equal Emphasis on Business Results and Individual Development*

Organizations have long relied on various groups to achieve results. From the earliest days of the Industrial Revolution, work groups reporting to the same supervisor have focused on meeting the requirements of their departments. In modern times, self-directed teams have become empowered to take initiative. In matrix organizations, workers may be involved with numerous projects at the same time. Learning how to deal with the stress created by competing time demands has grown to be an important skill for all workers and managers.

In traditional action learning, new teams are formed to carry out action learning projects to address a business need while also developing team members by exposing them to people, approaches, and resources from other departments, divisions, or geographical locations. The organization benefits by securing creative solutions to challenging business problems, training materials based on the collective perceptions of a team representing different organizational perspectives, or visions formulated from a broad perspective of a team representing diverse stakeholder groups within the organization.

Placing equal emphasis on business results and individual development means achieving measurable results in both areas targeted. Therefore, there are typically two facilitators on any action learning team. One member serves as a task leader to ensure business results are achieved. A second member is a team facilitator who ensures the team members work together harmoniously and learn from each other. The team facilitator can help to find resources the team needs to address team challenges.

In accelerated action learning, teams also have two team leads. They also focus on work tasks (achieving work results) and team relationships (learning and group cohesion). However, the team leader and team facilitator bear equal responsibility for ensuring that the team works at speed to get results.

Phase 7: *Complete the Action Learning Set*

In traditional action learning, the action learning set ends when the team encounters one limitation or constraint. Such limitations may include:

- Running out of time (the team was given a deadline during the initial briefing)
- Running out of resources (the team runs out of the budget established during the initial briefing)
- Solving the problem to the satisfaction of others (problem solved)
- Preparing the training materials to the satisfaction of others (training prepared, field tested, or delivered)
- Formulating the vision to the satisfaction of others (vision formulated and accepted)
- Meeting required business goals.

Completing the action learning set in accelerated action learning follows the abovementioned limitations. However, in each case, the team works to achieve results *faster*. Time pressure (and the coincident stress) is increased and is regarded as a tool to encourage team development. Time pressure can force individuals and groups to focus on how they approach issues efficiently and effectively and think about issues more creatively.

Phase 8: *Debrief the Action Learning Team Members Collectively*

Learning occurs through new experiences and reflection on those experiences. Therefore, focusing all attention on action alone is not good enough. At the end of an action learning set, the need exists to facilitate individual and group reflection on the learning experience(s).

Team facilitators may pose such questions as:

- Did you have a moment of realization?
- What did you learn?
- What do you believe the experience(s) revealed about your future learning or development needs?
- What are you proud of as a group?
- What could have improved group dynamics?
- How well did the team deal with time pressure, and how can stress be managed better?

In traditional action learning, questions like those listed above are typically posed in face-to-face groups. Team members reflect as a group on their experience.

In accelerated action learning, the questions are still posed. However, to speed up the process, which might otherwise be slowed down by the need to schedule times when all group members might get together, all team members are polled using collaborative technology that permits all team members to see what individual team members wrote. That can slash the time needed for group debriefs.

Phase 9: *Debrief the Action Learning Team Members Individually*

In traditional action learning, individual team members are also debriefed separately from the collective team debrief. That Phase is undertaken because sometimes individuals are uncomfortable talking about themselves in a group setting. There is a need to talk to each group member after an action learning set.

Those who speak to action learning team members individually may still ask the questions posed under Phase 8 above. However, they will direct the questions to individuals rather than to the group. In accelerated action learning, the same technique is used. However, as in Phase 8, virtual methods such as email, group chat, and other technology-assisted methods may speed up the debriefing process. Additionally, in accelerated action learningm team members are individually asked how they dealt with the stress created by time pressures and how they might improve their performance when under time pressure.

Phase 10: *Reassign Action Learning Team Members Based on Their Individual Development Needs*

By participating in action learning sets, team members may discover new development needs. Meeting those needs may require assigning them to new action learning sets or new work assignments to solve problems, address training challenges, formulate new visions, or achieve new goals.

In accelerated action learning, this Phase is the same as in the traditional sense. The only real difference is in the speed with which it occurs, as the teams are on a constant lookout on their own. This Phase is carried out quickly—often within a few hours of completing an action learning set.

When Should Accelerated Action Learning Be Used?

As in the case of traditional AL, AAL can be used when there is value to be gained by rapidly solving business problems and developing individuals and groups for the future. AAL is most appropriate when there is a pronounced need to meet time pressures. Time itself is a strategic resource, and meeting business needs in real time, while also building employee bench strength, is often a necessity. Putting people under time pressure to get results instills a sense of urgency in workers and managers alike. Interestingly, unlike traditional AL which should usually be avoided when time pressures are pressing, the AAL approach can overcome this challenge. In AAL, workers must perform under time pressure, and time itself becomes an important element in workers' developmental experiences. Workers learn how to cope with the stress that stems from performing at speed and learning in real time, while working.

However, accelerated action learning is not appropriate when:

■ The business challenge does not offer enough opportunities to learn
■ A dearth of relevant subject matter expertise exists within the organization or is available outside the organization
■ The people in leadership positions do not value employee opinions and do not value how important it is to develop individuals and/or teams to meet future business needs and cope with time pressures.

How Does Accelerated Action Learning Relate to the 70-20-10 Rule?

The 70-20-10 rule has grown popular in business circles. First introduced by Lominger and Associates, the notion is that planned onsite or online training should comprise only 10 percent of efforts to develop employees. More emphasis—about 70 percent—should be placed on developmental efforts integrated with the work. The idea is simple: workers learn more if they learn in the work context rather than in venues like training classrooms or onsite learning that are removed from the daily work. About 20 percent of all employee development should occur through peer interaction (either onsite or online through social media) or through social learning (watch and imitate).

Accelerated action learning sits at the apex of all three approaches to employee development. It can be planned and thus be part of the 10 percent; it can be integrated with daily work assignments and thus be part of the 70 percent; and, in any case, all action learning usually involves learning experiences that encourage people to learn from those in other functions (cross-functional exposure) or other cultures (cross-cultural exposure).

Alternative Approaches to Action Learning

Traditional action learning and accelerated action learning, as they are described in this chapter, are not the only ways to carry out action learning. An important alternative is widely practiced in the United Kingdom and other parts of the world outside of North America. It is described in the interview below.

EXHIBIT 1.2 AN INTERVIEW WITH THE CEO OF THE SCHOOL FOR SOCIAL ENTREPRENEURS INDIA

The School for Social Entrepreneurs (SSE) India launched in February 2016, a franchisee school of the SSE in the UK, and supported by PwC in India to set up the operations. The CEO of SSE India believes that action learning is the organization's backbone. SSE India has championed the use of action learning to help social entrepreneurs.

We chose this methodology as the backbone of all our programs to support social leaders because this approach can:

■ Enhance team working and collaboration skills
■ Develop problem-solving and decision-making skills
■ Create a solution to an organizational challenge which provides immediate benefits
■ Enhance ability to reflect on and learn from individual and collective experiences
■ Develop awareness of how individual behaviors, attitudes, and assumptions impact on decision-making.

Mr. Shalabh Mittal feels that the action learning pedagogy and approach to problem-solving is highly beneficial and gets accelerated naturally because people present their problems and the entire discussion is all about that. It cuts out the noise, which is why it accelerates naturally.

The participants in the set:

■ Really hear and listen to each other—to the words and the emotions
■ Allow for pauses and silence
■ Commit to attending the sessions and agreeing on dates in advance to help support attendance
■ Hold the content of what they talk about as confidential and agree not to discuss it with others outside of the AL team

- Take responsibility for their own learning and note their action points
- Are willing to honestly review their process and give feedback that supports the group's development
- Are willing to try things out and experiment and learn from them.

A robust group agreement lays the foundation to bring the culture of reflection and building self-awareness as the core of the action learning group and experience.

As advocates of action learning (AL), the SSE recognizes that, although this transformative process holds immense promise, it is not without its share of challenges. In the SSE experience, the organization has identified a few key hurdles that demand attention and careful navigation. By acknowledging and addressing these challenges, SSE can unlock the true potential of AL as a tool to solve complex personal and enterprise problems.

1) **Valuing the Process.** One significant challenge is that participants often need to recognize the true value of the AL process as a catalyst for personal and organizational transformation. Trust in the process is essential, and some individuals may hesitate to surrender themselves fully to its potential. The SSE task is to cultivate an understanding of the profound impact that AL can have on problem-solving and create an environment where participants can embrace the process wholeheartedly.

2) **Reinforcing Purpose and Ownership.** The purpose of AL must be continually reinstated and shared with the group. Sometimes, participants bring external problems to the session, seeking support and solutions for issues that do not directly concern them. It is vital to emphasize that the AL process revolves around the issue-holder and their specific challenge. Redirecting participants towards internal issues and encouraging ownership is crucial to maintaining the integrity and effectiveness of the AL experience.

"'Action Learning was hard to get a grasp of at first, but I am loving the process now. :)'—from one of our AL participants."

Shalabh Mittal
Chief Executive Officer
School for Social Entrepreneurs India

Ruth Cook, Founding Director, Action Learning Associates, In-depth Interview

Question 1: How do you define action learning? Please explain.

The typical approach to the action learning model in the UK—and in some other parts of the world—differs from the North American model, in which action learning consultants are invited into a company or work with a group of people to solve a business problem.

Our model is based on the model of Reg Revans, the founder of action learning. A Canadian colleague calls ours the "classic" or "pure" model.

It focuses on collaborating with a group of peers, a team, or the entire organization on a variety of issues. It could also be about bringing people from one or more organizations together to address the challenges they each individually face. Sometimes, these are complete strangers to each other's worlds, whereas, at other times, they may work in the same sector. It is less common for us to collaborate with people from the same organization to solve one single problem, although, when we are working with a group of peers from one organization, they often identify organizational action that is needed.

Question 2: How do you use action learning?

Let me describe the methodology. We bring together a group of people. They may be colleagues in the same organization, or they may even be strangers from different organizations. Typically, a group consists of six, seven, or eight people in a group who meet for a period. Sometimes, they meet every month for six months; at other times, they meet every couple of months for a year. But the relationship, once established, always persists for a period. I have had groups that have worked together for 20 years. Sometimes, people say there is no other space than these action learning groups where they get the opportunity for this type of thinking, action, and reflection. Participants in action learning really value their time in the groups, and they commit time to it. Those working virtually tend to devote three hours to their meetings. If they are working face-to-face, then they work together for half a day or the full day. They meet up for a full day because some of them must travel from various parts of the UK. For that reason, it is beneficial for them to make the best use of their time. An onsite group might meet for five days or five half-days over 12–15 months.

Let me describe how it works. In the first session, I describe the methodology, we have time getting to know each other through extended introductions, and I demonstrate the model and answer questions. At each subsequent session, people start by talking about what has happened to them since the last session. If they acted on a previous presentation between sessions, then they report on that.

Then we have a bidding round to agree on who would present a topic on that occasion. The first person begins his or her presentation—the challenge that they face and how they would like the group to help. Ideally, they can talk about this for as long as they want. Other participants in the session then ask them questions—first to clarify their understanding and then to ask open-ended questions. The core of the action learning process is open questions.

Unlike the North American model, we do not allow people to make any interventions other than questions. That means they cannot give advice, and they cannot share their own stories.

The questions then shift to action questions, with the speaker formulating a plan of action. We may record what the speaker says on a chart or a screen. The final stage is that each person offers the presenter some reflections. That is not about what the individual should do; rather, it is about "this is what I heard or how you came across." There are also opportunities for reflection and participants talk about their own learning. It is rare that a situation someone else describes generates no learning for others. There is usually some point that makes people think about what they do and how they respond. In short, people share that with each other and offer the presenter honest feedback on what they have heard.

After that, the next presenter shares an issue or a challenge that they face, and the entire process repeats.

From time to time, we would have a process review so that the group can reflect on how well they are doing and how they can improve.

Question 3: In this organization that you have started, people can register for such kinds of cohort. How are these groups formed?

People join a group. It is a closed group which meets over a period. They contract with each other to meet over four, five, or six sessions over an agreed-upon timespan. If it occurs inside an organization, then it would be organized in a similar way. Often, sensitive topics are the focus of attention for these groups and so confidentiality is very important.

An example of our work would be a university or a foundation that is running a fellowship scheme. They want all their participants in the fellowship scheme to go through action learning as a part of their development. Those cohorts would remain the same throughout the lifetime of the fellowship and they might choose to continue beyond that. We also recruit to stranger sets. But where it is a foundation, organization, or a company, they would put the sets together. Then we would brief people, explain the methodology, what they are committing to, and then they would meet for their sessions.

Question 4: Is it true that, in action learning, you are trying to solve a problem and simultaneously trying to develop people?

Yes. To add to that, sometimes, people bring a project or a decision that they must make or a career choice that they are making or how a team is functioning. So, it is not necessarily a business or a company problem.

Sometimes, the priority for the organization centers on the development opportunity. People may participate in action learning because it is a part of leadership development or because they want to get better at coaching skills. Quite often, action learning is used in an organization undergoing a culture change. In a way, action learning is also a part of the culture change. It encourages people to be more honest with each other or give feedback, creating more of a coaching culture. So, although action learning is creating coaching abilities for people, it is also a platform where they may talk about cultural transformation. For example, we have worked with civil service departments undergoing massive change. Their senior leaders require a safe space to discuss this, and action learning can help them do so.

More often than running action learning sets, we now train action learning facilitators. Our model of action learning is a skill that people can learn, and people can be in self-facilitating sets. We go into an organization and train their facilitators because it is more cost-effective than for them to rely on consultants to facilitate. If the facilitation training is done face to face, then it is typically delivered in a three-day program. If we deliver it online it is generally over 4 sessions.

Question 5: How often do organizations use virtual teams or virtual groups to solve problems?

During the pandemic, organizations used action learning for virtual groups all the time. Before that, we had been using virtual action learning for about eight years. In all, the experience base with virtual groups is over 12 years.

Because we have worked with many international organizations, they need to train cohorts of people across cultures. That usually requires virtual training for group members and virtual action learning groups.

Question 6: In the groups so formed, among the two leaders in it, is one focusing on the task at hand and the other focusing on the developmental needs and ensuring the smooth facilitation of the team performance, or what? What is the leadership model for an action learning team that works effectively?

We would just work with one facilitator on the team. But we also suggest that action learning works best if it is a group of peers. It is best if there is no line management relationship within the group. If you have a line manager in the group, this can be a potential impediment to group learning, as it can inhibit honest reflection. However, we have sometimes worked with teams that include the line manager—there has to be a high degree of trust.

Question 7: How successful is the peer-to-peer relationship model compared with the line manager model?

Highly successful. I think people feel the freedom to speak honestly. If people are part of an organization undergoing dramatic change, then there can also be important themes or messages that need to be fed back into the organization—with the agreement of the participants—but without breaking confidentiality. We would identify those issues, and we would report them back to the same senior management team or chief executive. We do not name who said what or talk about individuals; rather, we might say something like "all of your middle managers identify xyz as their biggest challenge."

Question 8: What is the difference between focus group discussions and action learning groups?

Action learning is a wonderful way for people to develop emotional intelligence. In action learning, participants work with a trusted group of peers where they can see how different people respond to different issues. It can really develop emotional intelligence.

A focus group brings people together to discuss a topic for a short period of time. You have a fixed number of questions. The focus group is over when the questions are asked and the answers are given. But, in action learning, the focus is not on questions posed in advance. The people generate the questions and the answers. The participants in action learning set the agenda.

Question 9: Do you find any similarity between this approach to action learning and appreciative enquiry?

People who have come to our programs to train as facilitators have sometimes also trained in appreciative inquiry. Appreciative inquiry enables them to ask certain types of questions that can be really useful.

Question 10: What would you say are the biggest challenges/problems that you run into when running action learning processes?

In the present business sector in the UK, the pressure is such that people want quick answers. They want to do everything quickly. Action learning does not always fit easily into that model. It is not a quick fix. People need to commit time to it. They need to be willing to invest in it. For example, when working virtually, we like to work in sessions of three hours. However, some companies claim that this is simply not possible. They say, "we cannot do anything that lasts for three hours." Sometimes, we have done action learning in two or two and a half hours. But to be honest, three hours is what you need. The reason for this is that it is a one-of-a-kind working style. People must slow down and become more reflective. They need to make time; they need to have silence between questions, and they may need to learn to work at a different pace. That is a big challenge for people. It can be difficult to create the time necessary for it. For example, we worked with an organization that is part of the health service. No matter how much they valued it, getting people away from their clinics for action learning groups proved impossible because they simply could not be released due to the pressures of their work.

Question 11: What are the biggest advantages or benefits realized using action learning groups or teams?

Action learning gives people protected time and a space for critical reflection. That is important at present since the pace of change is so great.

People simply do not have enough time to reflect on what they are doing, consider what they could do differently, and then change, according to David Kolb's learning cycle. That is what action learning can do. Action learning groups provide a structure for people to think about and reflect critically on what they are doing. They do this with their peers and consider what actions to take.

People, mostly at the senior level, get the feeling of not being alone. Those running organizations can find it difficult to find a place to discuss honestly how they respond to the challenges they face.

Another issue that can be addressed is the *imposter syndrome*. That means that people feel that they are imposters who are not adequately competent to do the jobs they are performing. Many women suffer from imposter syndrome. I have been amazed at very senior leaders who seem self-confident, but experience imposter syndrome. In action learning groups, people can talk honestly and confidentially about the feelings that arise from their role.

Question 12: How often do you, as a trainer/consultant, plan microlearning events? How do you plan them and take them to "best practices" form. How often do you benchmark how the organizations solve similar problems?

We are not currently using microlearning. The only training that we do is about action learning. We train new facilitators and give them an experiential program so that they can experience action learning. We also give them a way to practice facilitation over three days and then become facilitators in their own organizations.

Question 13: Do participants in action learning ever come back to you with feedback?

Yes. We do have a recognized program with the Institute of Leadership and Management (ILM). Following our training program, we asked participants to keep a reflective learning log. They write up reflections about their learning. Then, they come back after working with us, maybe six months later, and then they can become accredited with the institute by writing a log and sharing their experience with other people. The ILM has recognized this program. That organization is the body that runs many vocational courses in the UK. They also work internationally.

Question 14: What about reflection?

After someone has explored a topic or question in depth and come up with an action, then we encourage people to share their reflections with the presenter. We deliberately keep that open-ended and without much structure. We do not have a formal, planned model of reflection because what people want to say varies enormously. They might want to offer feedback or talk about their own learning or both, but we encourage them to take some time to think and offer something that comes from the heart. People need to feel safe when they share their reflections and feelings.

Question 15: As a facilitator, is your role primarily managing the tone, tenor, and emotion of the receiver and the giver?

Yes. And it is also to model it within the group. The facilitator holds the action learning group to a structure to make sure the group does not go off on a tangent.

Final Thoughts on Accelerating Action Learning

Since there is a lot of emphasis on speed and efficiency in AAL, a half-day workshop on time management and stress management can further enhance the AAL process for those participating in it.

Here are a few tips on time management:

- Prepare a list of activities that one engages in on a day-to-day basis
- Check the relevance of each activity
- Avoid any deviation from the pre-decided schedule
- Practice mindfulness in choosing tasks throughout the AAL project
- Delegate day-to-day repetitive tasks.

Here are a few tips on stress management:

- Prepare oneself for new learning
- Engage in self-talk about "why" s/he is a part of the AAL process
- Ask for support at home and at the office for more time off work to synthesize new learning, for reflection, and assimilation of new learning

- Engage actively with the set/team members to have a better understanding of how to conduct oneself
- Seek clarity whenever possible from facilitators or team members.

References

Dean, P. J. (1998). Action learning: An ethical addition to performance improvement—you can ask and you can argue. *Performance Improvement Quarterly, 11*(2), 3–4.

Dotlich, D., & Noel, J. (1998). *Action learning: How the world's top companies are re-creating their leaders and themselves.* Jossey-Bass.

Gabrielli, S., Kimani, S., & Catarci, T. (2006). The Design of Microlearning Experiences: A Research Agenda. In: T, Hug, M, Lindner, & P. A. Bruck, (Eds.), *Microlearning: Emerging Concepts, Practices and Technologies after E-Learning: Proceedings of Microlearning Conference 2005*: Learning & Working in New Media (pp. 45–53). Innsbruck, áustria: Innsbruck University Press.

Noorani, R. (2008). *Rapid prototyping: Principles and applications.* Wiley.

Exhibit 1.3 A Tool to Guide Accelerated Action Learning

Worksheet to Plan Accelerated Action Learning	
Directions: Use this worksheet to plan your Accelerated Action Learning set. For each issue described in the left-hand column below, describe in the right-hand column how the step can be carried out in an AAL project. There are no absolutely "right" or "wrong" answers to any of these issues; rather, the goal is to discover a project plan to guide the AAL set.	
Issue	How Can Each Step Be Carried Out? (List tasks for each step. Also, develop a responsibility chart to identify which team members will be responsible for each task and a Gantt chart to identify the timeline for completing the steps/tasks.)
1 **Select a business problem, training challenge, organizational vision, or business goal.** Describe clearly the issue and what measurable results are targeted for the Accelerated Action Learning Set.	

2	**Form a small group or team of people (of about 6–7 people) who meet two criteria: (1) each team member brings a skill that may be helpful in addressing the issue described in Step 1; and (2) each team member has a need to build his or her skills in the area of the Accelerated Action Learning Set.** Form the team and get clearance from the immediate supervisors of each team member to serve on the team. Make sure that the job performance on the team will "count" on each team member's performance review. List the team members.	
3	**Brief the team members on: (1) the issue described in #1 above; (2) limitations established on the resources (time, money, staff, solution parameters) for the project.** Make clear when—or under what conditions—the project will "sunset."	
4	**Establish measurable goals for the Accelerated Action Learning Set.** Make sure there are two sets of goals: (1) business goals; and (2) individual learning/development goals for employee development.	
5	**Encourage team members to experiment with solutions.** Let the team struggle to solve the problem while learning from each other in the process. Disband the Accelerated Action Learning Set only when: (1) the problem is solved, the vision is realized, the goal is achieved, or the business goal is achieved; OR (2) team members or management "gives up." Team members may pilot test one or many solutions so long as limitations are observed.	

6	**Place equal emphasis on business results and individual development.** Have a *Team Leader* (to focus on achieving results from the Action Learning Team) and a *Team Facilitator* (to focus on helping individuals to meet their individual development goals.)	
7	**Complete the Accelerated Action Learning Set.** Disband the team only when the problem is solved, the vision is formulated, the business goal is achieved, the change objectives are achieved—or team members/managers give up.	
8	**Debrief the Accelerated Action Learning team members collectively.** Ask Action Learning team members what they learned from their experience on the Action Learning team.	
9	**Debrief the Accelerated Action Learning team members individually.** Ask each Action Learning team member what he or she learned from his or her experience on the Action Learning team and what could be done to build competencies by future assignments.	
10	**Reassign Accelerated Action Learning team members based on their individual development needs.** Loop back to Step #1 and select appropriate issues on which to assign Action Learning team members.	
11	**The overall process (Steps 1–10 above)**	

Chapter 2

Phase 1: Selecting a Business Problem, Training Challenge, Organizational Vision, or Business Goal

What is the starting point for accelerated action learning? The first phase is to select a business problem, training challenge, organizational vision, or business goal (see Exhibit 2.1). This chapter focuses on the first phase of accelerated action learning. The chapter opens with a case story. It also examines when accelerated action learning should be used, lists and describes the steps to be taken to select an issue suitable for accelerated action learning, summarizes the role that microlearning can play in this phase, and reviews the roles that team leaders and team facilitators can play in this first phase. This chapter also examines how individual reflection plays a part in this phase, delineates how virtual and hybrid settings should be considered in this phase, lists common mistakes made in this phase, and offers tips on how to solve or avoid those common mistakes. The chapter ends with a tool suitable for on-the-job application, which provides practical help in how to select issues suitable for action learning.

DOI: 10.4324/9781003348658-2

The Accelerated Action Learning Model (AALM)

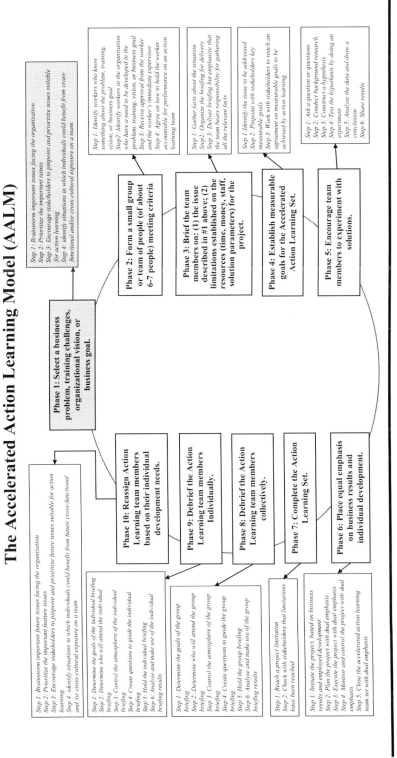

Exhibit 2.1   The Accelerated Action Learning (AAL) Model

Opening Case Story

Mary Norton is Vice President of Manufacturing for the Corregidor Corporation. Corregidor manufactures pipe fittings. It is a small company with about 300 workers. At its only location, in a small Midwestern city, the worker headcount of Corregidor fluctuates, depending on the time of year. During the warm season, which is also the peak for construction projects, Corregidor's employment numbers swell to 400 full-time workers and sometimes an additional 100 contingent workers.

Mary Norton has a problem with the assembly line. The rejection rate of pipe fittings on the assembly line has been on the increase. The reasons are a mystery. It is unclear whether the quality control problem stems from sleepy workers on the midnight shift, aging equipment on the assembly line, or many other reasons. Norton has limited time available to investigate on her own. She sees it as an opportunity to kill two birds with one stone: she will form an accelerated action learning team and invite workers in the organization to solve the problem, while also developing the workers involved.

Norton hand-picks seven workers for an accelerated action learning team. She asks them to meet during a noon break, and she picks up the tab for a pizza delivered to the conference room right off the assembly line where the problem is occurring. While the workers munch on pizza, Norton explains to them that she has an assignment for the group sitting in front of her. (She jokes that is the price they must pay for the pizza. That gets a few laughs.)

Norton briefly describes accelerated action learning as an approach that achieves two objectives at the same time. First, it brings together a team of workers that collectively possesses the knowledge, skills, and attitudes to solve a business problem, formulate a vision, achieve a business goal, or otherwise contribute to organizational success. Second, it also provides an opportunity to develop those workers. In this context, development means (1) giving the team members a chance to learn from others from different parts of the organization and build cross-functional knowledge; (2) giving team members in multinational companies a chance to learn from those based in other national cultures; and (3) providing a safe place for workers to innovate with new ideas and approaches, and inspire creativity in the work setting.

After a few questions from the workers, Norton appoints these people to the team:

- *Mary Wu*, whom Norton also appoints as team leader
- *Martin Wolfson*, whom Norton also appoints as team facilitator
- *Gordon Martin*, who comes from the company's marketing division
- *Loretta Nice*, who comes from the company's production division (and from the assembly line crew that works on the line with the quality problems)
- *Armena Phillips*, who comes from the company's HR division
- *Amanda Tinker*, who comes from the company's finance division
- *Ordana Links*, who comes from the company's production division but not from the assembly line with the quality control problem.

An important question to consider in this case story is this: *Is this situation appropriate for accelerated action learning?*

When Should Accelerated Action Learning Be Used?

As the opening case story indicates, accelerated action learning (AAL) can be used when the organization faces a problem and the workers in the organization can also benefit from development. Although managers could try to solve problems on their own without worker assistance, their efforts would not inspire buy-in and ownership from the workers. And, whereas worker development could be achieved that does not require accelerated action learning, AAL can be a most useful approach to encourage workers to learn from each other while also gaining some exposure to cross-functional views provided by representatives from different "siloes" within the organization. It should be used to build urgency and accelerate the process of innovation and solutions.

What Are the Steps to Select an Issue Suitable for Accelerated Action Learning?

Step 1: Brainstorm Important Issues Facing the Organization

Typically, the important issues facing the organization are identified by the leaders of the organization. They may come up with a short list of major issues worthy of exploration. Those important issues may be linked to the organization's strategic plan or may otherwise arise from daily challenges arising from the competitive environment.

As in the case story described at the opening of this chapter, projects appropriate for AAL may be chosen by senior organizational leaders or else by anyone in authority—such as team leaders, supervisors, or managers.

Step 2: Prioritize the Important Issues

Once important issues are identified, they must be prioritized. Which ones are worthy of investigation and experimentation? Although that is a matter of opinion, organizational leaders can identify what they believe to be the most important issues. They may be pressed to explain why some issues are more worthy of AAL than others.

Step 3: Encourage Stakeholders to Pinpoint and Prioritize Issues Suitable for Accelerated Action Learning

Once important issues have been identified and prioritized, then important stakeholders should consider what issues would be best addressed by AAL. Note that AAL is always focused on achieving three important outcomes: (1) business results; (2) individual and collective development of the AAL team members and (3) achieving the objectives at a faster pace with the help of enablers like microlearning and individual reflection'. Remove the inverted commas before achieving and the one towards the end.

Step 4: Identify Situations in Which Individuals Could Benefit from Cross-Functional and/or Cross-Cultural Exposure on a Team

Collective and individual development are of equal importance in AAL.

Organizations form many groups to achieve business results. These may include task forces, management committees, councils, advisory groups, steering committees, and even temporary groups, such as process improvement committees. But, in those experiences, the focus is primarily on achieving business results rather than emphasizing the collective or individual development of those on an AAL team.

Often, a major benefit of AAL teams is also cross-functional and cross-cultural exposure. In most organizations, individuals are hired in a silo (functional area) and may proceed up the chain of command during their careers. Often, they gain little exposure to the occupants of other siloes, unless placed on committees or task forces. However, AAL teams can be constructed to achieve both business results and cross-functional (or even cross-cultural) exposure. That exposure is important for those moving up the organizational chart to senior positions where they may oversee the actions of those in many different functional areas and in many geographic locations.

What Role Does Microlearning Play in This Phase?

Microlearning is understood to mean "bite-sized learning efforts." Interest in microlearning originally stemmed from the work of scholar Hermann Ebbinghaus in the 1880s on memory, while action learning stemmed from the work of Reg Revans in the 1940s. Ebbinghaus found that memory is not consistent and may vary depending on the topic/issue and on the learning and development methods used.

Much interest in microlearning exists because workers face genuine challenges in getting the time from their employers to participate in lengthy off-the-job training programs or in complicated on-the-job online learning programs. Few organizations have enough staff to free people up to attend development programs—unless they can somehow be integrated with onsite work. At the same time, the popularity of Lominger's well-known 70-20-10 rule indicates that about 70 percent of all development programs should occur on the job and be integrated with the work, 20 percent of all development programs should occur through interaction with other people (mentors, social media partners, and peers), and only 10 percent of development programs should occur through planned onsite, online, or blended learning experiences (Lombardo and Eichinger, 1996).

When thinking about AAL to solve a business problem, meet a training challenge, formulate an organizational vision, or achieve a business goal, microlearning can be used. Microlearning events typically include any method that can provide learning in a highly abbreviated fashion. Examples include:

- *Infographics*: one-page pictures that pack in much information
- *Real-time quizzes*: short quizzes
- *Microtext*: short text segments (one page or less) that provide information
- *Mobile apps*: computer programs that are short and provide real-time information
- *Social media support*: short text messages packed with useful examples or information

- *Short video segments*: five minutes or less
- *Games*: can be played in a few minutes
- *Screen-saver messages*: brief online messages can provide or inspire learning
- *Job aids*: one-page checklists, for example, can be offered to learners as they work.

The above list is not meant to be exhaustive; rather, it merely illustrates examples of microlearning methods.

These methods can be used when selecting a business problem, training challenge, organizational vision, or business goal. Microlearning can offer real-time information about:

- Who should be involved in AAL
- Which issues should be the focus of attention in AAL
- When AAL sets should begin and end
- Where AAL sets should be carried out and from what locations participants should be drawn
- Why AAL should be used in preference to other methods (such as training, coaching, and so forth)
- How the selection process of issues for AAL should be carried out.

What Are the Roles of Team Leaders and Team Facilitators in This Phase?

Team Leaders and team facilitators do not play a role in this first phase of the AAL model. The reason this phase does not call for roles from team leaders and team facilitators is that the action learning set has not yet been created, and working with an action learning team is the primary responsibility of team leaders and team facilitators.

How Is Reflection Used in This Phase?

Reflection is defined as the process of serious thought or consideration. In Kolb's learning cycle model of experiential learning, reflection plays an important part (Kolb, 1983). For Kolb, a concrete experience should be followed by reflective observation, which means to reflect on the experience that the individual or group has had (Kolb based his views on John Dewey's belief that learning stems from experience). Based on concrete experience, individuals or groups can draw conclusions from the experience and can then formulate future experiments that can give rise to future concrete experiences.

In AAL, it is important not just to solve a business problem, meet a training challenge, formulate, or act on an organizational vision, or achieve a business goal, but also to encourage reflection at every stage of the ten-step AAL model. Each challenge is a basis for concrete experience. But, when selecting a problem, dealing with a training challenge, formulating a vision, or achieving a business goal, selecting that issue is itself a concrete experience.

How can reflection be used in this phase? The answer is that decision-maker(s) involved in choosing when AAL should be used will, by necessity, need to reflect on whether the issue warrants AAL. Reflection can be stimulated by:

■ Thinking about whether AAL is appropriate for a situation
■ Thinking about the people to be developed and what practical work challenges will yield the best learning opportunities, given what those people need to learn about
■ Keeping a log to record the decision-maker's thoughts and direct those thoughts to occasions when AAL might be appropriate
■ Encouraging decision-makers who contemplate using AAL to ask themselves why that approach might be appropriate
■ Inviting workers to offer thoughts on what issues might warrant the application of AAL
■ Asking questions of workers, once they understand what AAL is, as to whether they believe AAL is appropriate
■ Using mind maps to guide reflection on AAL, or else using mind maps when thinking about an organizational problem, a training issue, an organizational vision, or a business goal to be achieved.

Any of the approaches above may stimulate reflection during the phase of selecting on which issues to focus AAL. Even games, of growing popularity in talent development, can be used to build AAL team engagement and stimulate reflection.

EXHIBIT 2.2 HOW MAY ORGANIZATIONS BENEFIT FROM USING AN AAL TEAM TO DESIGN TRAINING?

A recent trend called "Gamification" is a unique tool to create benefits using the AAL team to design training. Gamification uses game techniques and aspects in non-game contexts, including training or education. Gamification can boost motivation, engagement, knowledge, and skill retention in group learning. Gamification can be applied to group instruction through badges, points, leaderboards, missions, and quests.

Gamification can be used to make AAL engaging. The tool "Leaderboard," for example, helps keep the participants engaged and makes them want to give their best to emerge victorious in a unique learning environment. The larger group is divided into teams. Each team competes to score the highest on the pre-defined winning metrics (linked to metrics such as "service improvisation").

The simulated environment helps create a safe environment where participants can make mistakes and learn from them without costing the company any financial or other losses. Customized scenarios help make the learning most relevant, and the learning can be applied immediately back on the job. This approach can be used for service improvisation but can be applied to any other area in a business, like sales, leadership, finance for non-finance, operations, etc.

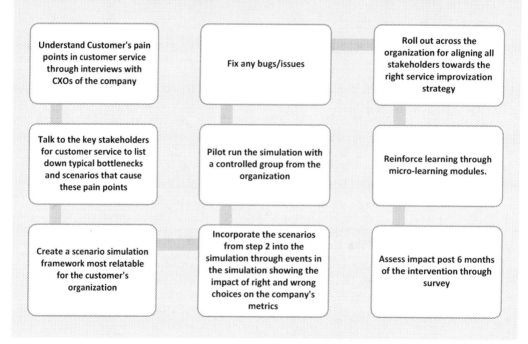

STEPS TO CREATE A GAMIFICATION BOARD GAME TO BE USED FOR AAL

Find below a worksheet for AAL practitioners using the gamification board game.

Stage 1:

- What are the critical pain points affecting customer service in your organization?
- Why would addressing them be critical for you?
- What are the metrics used to evaluate customer service within the organization?
- What would be the ideal numbers for these metrics?

Stage 2:

- What are some typical scenarios you encounter for factor X affecting customer service within your organization?
- What are some behaviors/processes you would like to modify in order to improve customer service within your company?
- Are there any industry factors that affect customer service in your organization?
- Are there any competitor strategies that could affect customer service in your organization?

Stage 3:

- This involves creating a bare-bones scenario simulation structure for the industry for which the simulation is created, with branched scenarios.

Stage 4:

- This involves creating a scenario simulation with the above scenarios through stages 1 and 2. Winning metrics are defined through the metrics obtained through stage 1.

(*Shared by co-founders Mr. Ronak Moondra, Mrs Harsha and Ms. Bhargavi Upadhyaya of "Imperium Edutech," a learning and development organization based in India.*)

What Should Be Considered for Virtual and Hybrid Settings in This Phase?

Where and how AAL is carried out can influence the quality of the experience. Traditionally, action learning has been conducted face-to-face. However, in recent years, and exacerbated by the pandemic, many organizations were forced to experiment with virtual AAL or else make use of hybrid experiences in which some of those participating in action learning were in a central office whereas others participated from their homes. Working in online or hybrid groups can change group dynamics. It is easier to have informal interactions—talking about us and our off-the-job experiences—when participants are in small, face-to-face groups (Rothwell and Park, 2021).

According to well-known media guru Marshall McLuhan (1994), "The media is the message." By that famous quote, McLuhan indicated that how a message is delivered can shape the meaning of that message. The way a message is delivered can change its meaning. Much of human communication depends on issues that go beyond the words spoken or written. According to theorist Albert Mehrabian in a classic research study (Mehrabian and Ferris, 1967), 55 percent of communication is non-verbal, 38 percent is verbal, and 7 percent consists of words only. As much as 40 percent of communication is conveyed vocally through tone and inflection.

Allan and Barbara Pease (2006) looked at thousands of recorded sales conversations from the 1970s and 1980s in *The Definitive Book of Body Language* and discovered that body language accounted for most of the negotiating influence. They also considered how, in phone discussions, the individual with the strongest argument usually prevails—but not always in face-to-face conversations. A person's body language and initial impressions can affect decision-making. Body language can also reveal information about a person's emotional state. For example, even if they claim otherwise, you already know that someone who crosses their arms is guarded or dissatisfied. Reading body language is like learning a second language and can assist in distinguishing perception from reality.

Jeff Thompson (2011) suggests that we might improve our ability to read non-verbal signals by remembering the three Cs of non-verbal communication: *context*, *clusters*, and *congruence*. *Congruence*, which is the comparison of spoken words to body language and tone. Using *context* means having a deeper knowledge of the situation. Knowing that someone suffers from anxiety, for example, can explain why they appear anxious during a fireworks display. Finally, employing *clusters* means influencing the interpretation of a person's body language by using many expressions or movements, rather than a few.

How Can This Phase Be Evaluated?

Evaluation is important in all areas of learning and development. Managers in many companies often ask for evidence that learning interventions work and provide a positive return on investment.

But how is the selection of AAL evaluated?

The answer to that simple question could fill books.

However, two major criteria govern the evaluation of AAL. First, is the choice of the challenge confronting the AAL team appropriate? Was the problem worth solving, was the training worth developing, was the vision worth formulating and/or implementing, or was the goal worthy of achieving? Second, are the team members developed appropriately by working together on the AAL team?

Avoiding the Most Common Mistakes

Several mistakes are common in this phase.

One mistake is to select AAL to address issues that do not warrant AAL. Examples would be simple decisions that require little investigation or decisions about which few people care. As a simple example, suppose an organization's leaders were weighing work-from-home options. Management had narrowed the choices to only two: either work three days in the office and two from home, or work two days in the office and three from home. In that example, the decision is so narrow that workers who participated in AAL would only feel frustrated by the lack of flexibility given to them in their experiments. To correct that problem, management would need to have a broader array of options and allow workers on AAL teams to experiment with the differences in productivity and worker engagement that might result from other choices.

A second mistake is for decision-makers to select AAL but start with an unwillingness to give the AAL team sufficient time, money, or other resources to apply AAL properly. That can happen when fad-crazed decision-makers believe they can get something for nothing. They have heard about AAL and find the idea intriguing but are unwilling to commit to the issue with those AAL teams they form. As a simple example, suppose decision-makers in an organization tasked a worker team to examine different approaches to recruiting staff. Management gave the workers a deadline of two weeks! That would not be sufficient time to obtain credible results!

References

Ebbinghaus, H. (1885). *Memory: A contribution to experimental psychology.* Dover.

Kolb, D. (1983). *Experiential learning: Experience as the source of learning and development* (2nd ed.). Prentice-Hall.

Lombardo, M., & Eichinger, R. (1996). *The career architect development planner* (1st ed.). Lominger.

McLuhan, M. (1994). *Understanding media: The extensions of man* (Reprint ed.). MIT.

Mehrabian, A., & Ferris, S. R. (1967). Inference of attitudes from nonverbal communication in two channels. *Journal of Consulting Psychology, 31*(3), 48–258.

Pease, A., & Pease, B. (2006). *The definitive book of body language: The hidden meaning behind people's gestures and expressions.* Bantam.

Revans, R. (1982). *The origins and growth of action learning.* Studentlitterattur.

Rothwell, W., & Park, C. (Eds.). (2021). *Virtual coaching to improve group relationships: Process consultation reimagined.* Routledge.

Thompson, J. (2011, September 30). Is nonverbal communication a numbers game? https://www.psychologytoday.com/us/blog/beyond-words/201109/is-nonverbal-communication-numbers-game

Exhibit 2.3 A Tool for How to Select Issues Suitable for Accelerated Action Learning

Directions: Use this tool to organize your thinking about selecting issues suitable for accelerated action learning. For each question appearing in the left-hand column below, place your answer in the right-hand column. It may be wise to involve several people in crafting the answers to the questions posed in the left-hand column. There are no "right" or "wrong" answers to the questions in any absolute sense, but some answers might be better than others under the circumstances.

Questions		Answers
1	Have your organizational leaders brainstormed on important issues facing the organization?	
2	Have the leaders of your organization prioritized the important issues listed in response to question 1 above?	
3	Have the organization's stakeholders been encouraged to pinpoint and prioritize issues suitable for accelerated action learning?	
4	Have your leaders identified situations in which individuals could benefit from cross-functional and/or cross-cultural exposure of a team?	
5	Can you describe the situation (problem, training, vision, or goal) and justify why accelerated action learning may be the best choice by which to address the situation?	

Chapter 3

Phase 2: Forming a Small Group or Team of People (of About 6–7 People) Meeting Criteria

What is the second phase of the accelerated action learning model (AALM)? The second phase is to form a small group or team, typically of about six to seven people who have skills that will aid them in solving a business problem, meeting a training challenge, formulating, or implementing a vision, or achieving a business goal. This chapter focuses on the second phase of accelerated action learning (see Exhibit 3.1).

This chapter opens with a case story about group or team selection. It also examines when accelerated action learning should be used, lists and describes the steps to be taken to select an issue suitable for accelerated action learning, summarizes the role that microlearning can play in this phase, and reviews the roles that team leaders and team facilitators can play in this second phase. The chapter also examines how individual reflection plays a part in this phase, delineates how virtual and hybrid settings should be considered in this phase, lists common mistakes made in this phase, and offers tips on how to solve, or avoid, those common mistakes. The chapter ends with a tool suitable for on-the-job application, and that tool provides practical help in how to select issues suitable for action learning.

DOI: 10.4324/9781003348658-3

The Accelerated Action Learning Model (AALM)

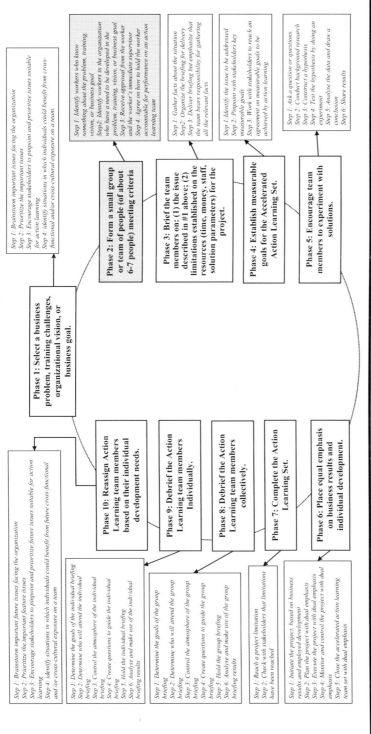

Exhibit 3.1   The Accelerated Action Learning Model (AALM)

Opening Case Story

Pam Arlan is an assistant store manager in a boutique women's clothing store in a mall in a southern US city. She has about five clerks who work for her in the store. They hold down the day shift at the store, but other part-time workers come in and work from 7 p.m. to 10 p.m. every day. Arlan's workers have reliefs, clerks who work part-time to give the full-time clerks their days off.

Arlan has a problem. The store is in trouble. The days when teenagers came into the store with their parents' credit cards and, without a moment's thought, bought expensive clothing seem to be over. The store has experienced major erosion of market share by such retailers as Walmart, Amazon, and other online retailers.

Arlan plans to assemble an AAL team to generate new ways for the store to make money. She wants to focus the AAL team on one idea at a time. The first idea is how to generate more foot traffic into the store, since she knows that sales always follow foot traffic. The second idea is how to position the store's clothing in more appealing ways so shoppers will be tempted to purchase the most attractive—and the most expensive—clothing as they walk around the store. The third idea is how to host events inside the store to generate publicity for the store.

A store like Arlan's has a flat organization chart. There are few management-level employees. Most workers are full-time or part-time clerks. Arlan puts her best clerks on the AAL team that will focus on the first idea. That team will include:

■ Marla Mapes, who has worked in the store since it opened in the mall in 1999
■ Gordon Sanders, who is a new hire with six months' experience
■ Hafesta Johnson, who has three years of experience in the store
■ Phoebe Knox, who joined the store one year ago as a contingent worker on the 7-to-11 shift
■ Buster Smith, who is also a contingent worker on the 7-to-11 shift.

An important question to consider in this case story is this: *How should an AAL team be formed, and what people should serve on the team?* Arlan also wonders how best to choose people for the team. She did not ask for volunteers; rather, she selected people she believed could provide the best information to solve the problems she saw and could also benefit from the development that the AAL team's experience would provide.

What Are the Steps to Forming a Group Suitable for Accelerated Action Learning?

Step 1: Identify Workers Who Know Something About the Problem, Training, Vision, or Business Goal

The first question to answer in Phase 2 is this: *Do the workers chosen for participation on an AAL team possess skills relevant to the issue for which the team was formed?*

Suppose, for example, that the AAL team formulates a vision of what the company should look like as a high-performance workplace. Each member should thus have skills relevant to that assigned issue. What skills would visioning require? Most likely, visioning would require entrepreneurial skills, since entrepreneurs are good at spotting future opportunities. AAL team members might also need to possess some data-gathering skills—such as abilities to conduct interviews, focus groups, and surveys—since visioning might require gathering information from the organization's workers.

Step 2: Identify Workers in The Organization Who Have a Need to Be Developed in the Problem, Training, Vision, or Business Goal

The second question to answer in Phase 2 is this: *Do the workers chosen for participation on an AAL team possess needs for development that could be met by participating in an AAL team?*

If the AAL team formulates a vision about what the company should look like as a high-performance workplace, then team members should need to develop visioning skills. By participating on the AAL team, they will develop that skill through the team experience.

Step 3: Receive Approval from the Worker and the Worker's Immediate Supervisor

Participating on an AAL team can be a part-time (a few hours a week) or a full-time (released from the worker's job for full-time participation) experience. Workers should not be coerced into AAL team participation. Nor should their immediate supervisors be forced to give up a worker desperately needed in their department or location. It is necessary to seek approval both from workers and from the workers' immediate supervisors. They should willingly agree to participate.

Step 4: Agree on How to Hold the Worker Accountable for Performance on an Action Learning Team

Accountability refers to a willingness to accept responsibility for action.

If workers accept placement on an AAL team, they also accept responsibility for participating on the team and working to meet the challenges posed to the team. If they fail in that responsibility, there must be consequences for them. And if they are distracted from team responsibilities because their immediate supervisor does not give them the time, money, or resources to participate after willingly granting participation, then there must be some way to hold that immediate supervisor accountable.

Many organizations use pay as a method of accountability. Workers who meet or exceed their job expectations are rewarded with pay increases or bonuses; workers who fall below their key performance indicators are punished by receiving lower pay increases or bonuses.

Establish some way to hold the members of AAL teams accountable for their work on the teams. If they are not held accountable, then they will likely not perform.

What Role Does Microlearning Play in This Phase?

Recall that microlearning simply refers to learning experiences organized in "bite-sized" segments. A general rule of thumb is that any learning experience of less than five minutes can be qualified as microlearning. As mentioned earlier, that includes infographics, some phone apps, some games, and short texts.

In this phase of accelerated action learning, microlearning can be organized around choosing people to serve on AAL teams. Prospective AAL team members may be chosen by managers, may be volunteers, or may represent some hybrid of volunteers who meet management requirements.

An application to serve on an AAL team may be required for participation. If that application has some learning element to it—that is, it requires the applicants to learn something—it could qualify as microlearning. For example, suppose a worker is encouraged by his or her manager to apply to serve on an AAL team. The worker might not know what AAL is and may thus be encouraged to discover. That could be a microlearning event if the worker/learner seeks more information about AAL.

At the same time, the challenge posed by the AAL event might also provide a learning opportunity for a prospective AAL team member. For example, suppose an AAL team is tasked to reinvent the company's job posting system. Team members may start their time on the team with little or no knowledge of job posting. To organize a new approach to job posting, AAL team members would find it necessary to investigate more about job posting. In doing so, they may do web searches on job posting, calling people about job posting, reading articles about job posting, and engaging in many activities that would enhance their knowledge of job posting. In doing so, they would engage in learning projects that would give them a base of knowledge they lacked on the topic.

What Are the Roles of Team Leaders and Team Facilitators in This Phase?

In the second phase of AAL, team leaders and team facilitators would probably not play any role. The reason is simple enough: the team in phase two has not yet been formed and therefore no team leaders or team facilitators exist for the team.

How Is Reflection Used in This Phase?

Perhaps learner reflection plays a limited role in the second phase of the AAL model because the AAL team has yet to be formed. Individual team members have not yet been selected, and the team does not yet exist until this phase is completed.

However, reflection may occur in this phase among managers considering people for participation on an AAL team, among those individuals who are asked to participate on an AAL team, or else are contemplating participating voluntarily on an AAL team.

Managers considering people for AAL team participation must weigh up two questions carefully as they reflect on those to select for an AAL team:

- Does the individual possess useful and necessary skills to solve the problem, meet the training challenge, formulate, or implement the vision, or achieve a goal needed for the AAL set?
- Does the individual need to be developed in an area that will be a focus of the AAL team project?

To reflect on the first question, managers must weigh up not only the skills on the topic of the problem to be addressed by AAL (such as job posting, in the example above) but also any investigatory skills needed (such as information retrieval skills, survey skills, statistical skills, and so forth) needed to carry out the AAL set successfully. An AAL team needs two kinds of skills: those related to the project; and those related to experimenting to find innovative ways to solve a problem, meet a training challenge, formulate, or implement a vision, or achieve a work goal/result.

To reflect on the second question, workers who consider volunteering for an AAL team must think about how much the AAL set might contribute to their short-term promotion prospects or their long-term career goals. As a simple example, an engineer thinking about participating on an AAL team tasked with discovering a different approach to job posting might be inclined to do it if the engineer is interested in shifting career paths away from engineering and moving into Human Resources. The reason: it is a way to develop the engineer to grow more familiar with an important HR-related topic.

What Should Be Considered for Virtual and Hybrid Settings in This Phase?

As noted in previous chapters, not all AAL teams work face to face. One reason is that many jobs are remote. Consider: "According to Upwork, one in every four Americans are working remotely in 2021, accounting for 26% of the American workforce. Upwork also predicts that, by 2025, 22% of the workforce (36.2 million Americans) will be working remotely ('Statistics on remote workers that will surprise you,' 2022"). According to *Forbes*, the pandemic of 2020–2021 has increased the likelihood that online workers will be from different cultures around the globe because online work has been made easier by the increased use of telework ("Cross cultural communication in a post-Covid world," 2023).

Due to the increased use of remote work, an increased percentage of AAL teams will likely make use of virtual and hybrid methods. It may add more issues for consideration when selecting (or considering) who to choose for participation on an AAL team. Among important issues to consider are:

◼ How much does each member of a possible AAL team possess the technology skills to work remotely if virtual or hybrid work on an AAL team is necessary? Do team members have (1) the appropriate equipment; (2) internet speed; and (3) technology skills to work together in a hybrid or virtual method?

■ Does each team member have the willingness to work on a team in a virtual format? A hybrid format?

■ Does each team member have the willingness to work with those from other races, genders, backgrounds, or cultures? That is understood to mean adequate emotional intelligence and cross-cultural competence.

It could be argued those who do not possess the willingness to work on a virtual or hybrid team or who do not possess the emotional intelligence or cross-cultural competence would stand to benefit most from the developmental opportunity afforded by participation on an AAL team. Working with those from widely diverse backgrounds may be the best way to develop people to work cross-culturally or cross-functionally (Rothwell et al., 2022).

How Can This Phase Be Evaluated?

Perhaps the best way to evaluate Phase 2 is to invite evaluation of the choice of team members before, during, and after the launch of an AAL team.

To evaluate before the formation of an AAL team, ask the manager(s) who selected team members why the team members were chosen. If they were chosen for appropriate reasons—they can contribute to the challenge posed to the AAL team and each member stands to be developed by participation—then the choice of members is appropriate. If, however, members were chosen for other reasons, then their participation may not be appropriate.

To evaluate the AAL team effort, simply survey team members at regular intervals about the team's performance. Do team members feel they collectively and individually possess the skills to meet the challenge of the team? Do team members feel they collectively and individually stand to benefit through the development experience that the team participation will afford? If the answers to these questions are "No," then it may be necessary to reconsider the team's membership even as the AAL team seeks to achieve team goals.

To evaluate after the AAL team effort, ask the AAL team members collectively and individually if they believe they were properly chosen for participation on the team. Ask them these questions: (1) Do you feel the team had the skills for the AAL project? (2) Do you individually feel you had one or more skills suitable for the AAL project? (3) Do you feel the team members benefited from the AAL team project by developing their individual and collective skills?

If AAL team members indicate that they were not chosen appropriately for the team experience, ask them:

- Why do you believe so?
- In what ways was your placement on the team inappropriate? Were you lacking necessary skills?
- Were you lacking development needs?

Take note of team members' answers. Consider their answers when making choices for participation on future AAL teams.

Avoiding the Most Common Mistakes

What could go wrong when managers select team members or when team members volunteer to participate on AAL teams?

There are several reasons members might be chosen for the wrong reasons. Managers may have workers they wish to get away from the workplace. Perhaps those workers are disruptive and do not get along with the manager or their co-workers; perhaps those workers are not performing adequately, and the manager would rather avoid conflict by placing them on a team away from the job; perhaps the workers are involved in problematic activities (the managers suspect them of something but cannot prove it) and the manager would rather remove those workers from their jobs.

Workers may be chosen for the wrong reasons to serve on AAL teams. That can destroy the credibility of AAL in the organization if left unchecked. Team leaders and team facilitators, once chosen, should monitor whether team members are chosen for their skills and developmental needs.

References

Cross cultural communication in a post-Covid world: The basics are as important as ever. (2023, March 22). https://www.forbesindia.com/article/thunderbird/cross-cultural-communication-in-a-postcovid-world-the-basics-are-as-important-as-ever/83833/1

Rothwell, W., Ealy, P., & Campbell, J. (Eds.). (2022). *Rethinking organizational diversity, equity, and inclusion: A step-by-step guide for facilitating effective change*. Routledge.
Statistics on remote workers that will surprise you. (2022, December 2). https://www .apollotechnical.com/statistics-on-remote-workers/

A Tool for An Application for an Accelerated Action Learning Team

The tools that follow can help to identify people for accelerated action learning teams. Exhibit 3.2 is an application form for individuals to apply for an AAL team.

Exhibit 3.2 An Application for an Accelerated Action Learning Team

Directions: This form will serve as your application to the AAL team. Management has provided the information in Part I. Please review this information carefully and then complete Part II. After this application is received, it will be reviewed by a panel of experts. You will be notified by [date] whether you have been selected to serve on the AAL team.

Your name _____

Today's date _____

The Accelerated Action Learning Team will focus on (briefly describe):

Part I
(To be filled out by the management)

1. What is the issue, problem, goal, or vision that will be the focus of the AAL team effort?

2. What knowledge and skill will most likely be needed by an AAL team member?

3. What will be the expected outcomes of participation on the AAL team regarding business and individual developmental outcomes?

4. What are the terms of the assignment on the AAL team?

Part II

(To be completed by the applicant)

Your Name	Your Job Title	Today's Date
Your Company Address	Your Phone Number	

1. What knowledge and skills do you possess that will contribute to the team achieving its desired outcomes? *Clarify your education, training, experience, or other qualifications.*

2. Why do you believe you need to work toward the individual developmental outcomes expected from this AAL project? *Clarify why you think you need this developmental experience regarding your career goals.*

3. How do you know that you can meet the terms of the assignment on the AAL team?

Chapter 4

Phase 3: Briefing Team Members About the Accelerated Action Learning Set

What is the third phase of the accelerated action learning model (AALM)? The third phase is to brief the Accelerated Action Learning (AAL) team on what is known about the problem the team is tasked to address, the vision the team is tasked to formulate or realize, the training the team is tasked to design and develop, or the goal the team is tasked to achieve (see Exhibit 4.1). Briefings may be performed by managers who have requested help to address an issue of concern. AAL team members may have to do their own investigation of a vaguely understood problem, training need, vision, or goal. If the latter is the case, then the team members must undertake an exploration of the problem. When that exploration is completed, the AAL team may have to brief management on what they discovered.

It is not unusual for an AAL team to be formed to address a problem that consists merely of the symptoms of a different underlying issue. For example, suppose management faces record turnover in the organization. Management may request an AAL team to be formed to address the turnover. But, in this example, turnover is merely a symptom—that is, a consequence—of some other, different root cause that is the underlying issue. In this example, turnover would be called the *presenting problem* because it is what appears (presents) and prompts management attention. But action to

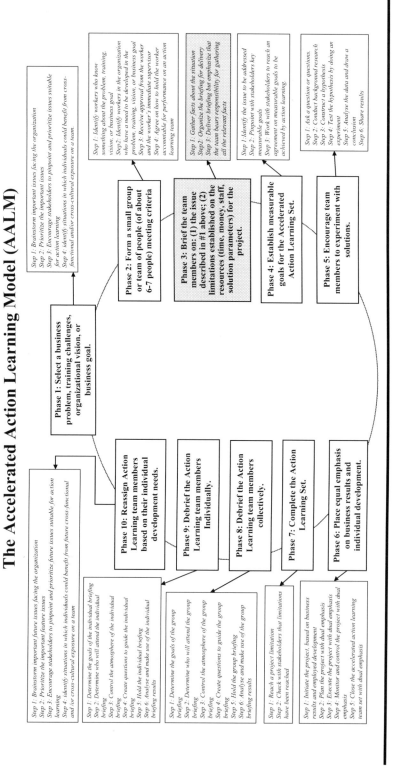

Exhibit 4.1   The Accelerated Action Learning Model (AALM)

address turnover without more efforts into identifying the underlying problems will mean treating symptoms rather than the cause of the "disease." Medical doctors would call it malpractice to treat the symptoms of physical ailments without regard to their underlying causes. This chapter focuses on the third phase of accelerated action learning.

This chapter opens with a case story about an AAL briefing situation. The chapter explores how briefings can be organized, summarizes the role that microlearning can play in this phase, and reviews the roles that team leaders and team facilitators can play in this third phase. The chapter also examines how individual reflection plays a part in this phase, delineates how virtual and hybrid settings should be considered in this phase, lists common mistakes made in this phase, and offers tips on how to solve, or avoid, those common mistakes. The chapter ends with a tool suitable for on-the-job application, and that tool provides practical help in how to select issues suitable for action learning.

Opening Case Story

The Bold Corporation faced a problem. Bold is a car dealership in the Northwestern United States. It is a large dealership with over one hundred car salespeople and a large central office staff of about 50 people.

Renatta Williams is the President and owner of Bold. She faces a problem with car sales. The inventory keeps growing as the car manufacturers send products (cars) to her dealership and demand payment. But customers are not buying the cars fast enough to get them off the car lot. The result is that Renatta's dealership risks bankruptcy. Her dealership must pay the manufacturer for the cars and then find a place to park/store them until a customer purchases them.

There are several problems in this situation. The first is that the cars are arriving faster than they are being sold. The second is that building an inventory of expensive cars requires substantial capital, and that means Renatta must borrow money from banks to buy the cars at high interest rates. Once the cars are purchased, they must be stored somewhere. Renatta's dealership does not have enough parking space for all the cars. Although Renatta could rent space to park the cars, the rental lots are usually far removed from the major streets. Most car dealers want their cars for purchase parked on lots that face busy streets so drivers can see the cars—and get interested enough to drive into the dealership, look at the cars, and purchase them.

Renatta has decided this business problem would be a good one to be addressed by an AAL team. She assembles a team consisting of two salespeople, two central office staff, and the dealership's service manager (who oversees car repairs and prepares new cars for purchase after factory arrival). Renatta briefs the AAL team herself. But she must decide what to tell them. It is important, Renatta feels, to cite specific facts about the problems. For instance, she wants to present the team with answers to questions like these: (1) how much does a new car, arriving from the factory, cost the dealership? (Prices vary by car model.); (2) how much has the dealership spent on arriving cars over the past year compared to how many cars were sold last year? (3) how much parking space for new cars does the dealership have, and how much parking space is being rented by the dealership? (4) how long, on average, does a new car sit in a parking lot before it is purchased? (5) what is the cost of interest paid to banks on all the new cars that the dealership purchased over the past year? (6) what debt does the dealership owe to banks, and how does that debt compare to the annual revenue of the dealership?

Renatta is sure that the AAL team will ask other questions about the problems. She is trying to gather as much information as she can before delivering the briefing, but she is sure the team will have questions she cannot answer.

What Are the Steps in Briefing an Accelerated Action Learning Team on an Issue?

Step 1: Gather Facts About the Situation

The sponsor of the AAL team should gather facts about the situation for organizing the AAL team briefing.

If *team sponsors*—a term used to refer to the individual or group that supports the AAL team—know about the problem, training challenge, vision, or goal, they use that information to prepare an evidence-based briefing about the issue. It is not expected that the team sponsors will have all the information and so it is likely that the AAL team, once formed, may have to investigate further, after an initial briefing, to gather more facts before solving the problem, meet the training challenge, formulate or implement a vision, or achieve a goal.

Step 2: Organize the Briefing for Delivery

After the AAL team members have been identified—either through management nomination and approval or through individual team member application and approval—the team sponsor will organize the briefing for delivery.

More information about organizing a concise, well-organized briefing appears below. But, for now, note that most briefings are presented to the AAL team and are typically one hour or less in length. Often, those briefings are videotapes for later viewing by AAL team members or others in the organization who may have interest in the AAL team's experiments.

Step 3: Deliver the Briefing but Emphasize That the Team Bears Responsibility for Gathering All Relevant Facts

Whenever the authors have delivered briefings, we have found that the question-and-answer session at the end of the briefing is filled with questions that usually require additional investigation beyond the initial briefing. Often, AAL team members will ask questions centering on "Why is that problem happening?" The team sponsors rarely know the complete answer, and additional work is usually necessary to gather essential information. And that should be the role of the AAL team. That point needs to be emphasized to AAL team members.

What Role Does Microlearning Play in This Phase?

Microlearning can play a role in a team briefing—both in preparing and in delivering the briefing.

When preparing a briefing on a business problem, a training challenge, a vision to be formulated or implemented, or a business goal to be achieved, microlearning can accelerate the time it takes for AAL team members to learn about the background. Microlearning is itself a strategy that can speed up familiarity with an issue, as are other methods (Hollins, 2022).

Recall that microlearning might include:

■ A quick web search to investigate an issue
■ A phone call to a friend to see if he/she has information about the issue or related issues
■ A social media call (like a posting to LinkedIn or to special groups on Facebook) to request information or even solutions and resources from anyone who reads the call (example: post to request information about onboard programs and receive examples from other organizations)
■ An infographic that might be uncovered by an image search on Google
■ Apps that might be available in the Apple store or other sites.

Rather than get background information from a lengthy process, such as reading a book or attending an onsite or online training program, AAL team members may get valuable background on global best practices or even common business practices through quick methods of gathering information. That information can craft a useful briefing for AAL team members.

Managers who will brief an AAL team should follow simple rules:

■ Do not provide all the information in the briefing. Make the AAL team take responsibility for providing missing or essential information. Just give the team what you know about the problem.
■ Try to answer basic questions at the briefing: (1) who is experiencing the issue that gives rise to the need for the AAL team project? (2) what is the issue, defined as best the manager can? (3) when did the issue/problem begin? (4) where does the issue/problem appear to most effect, i.e., where is the greatest pain? (5) why does the issue/problem exist, to the best of your knowledge? and (6) what efforts have been made to address the issue, and what results were obtained from those early efforts? Answer any other questions that may seem appropriate.

When delivering the briefing, managers—or AAL team members who have investigated the issue before the briefing—could apply the principles of microlearning by:

■ Using infographics in the presentation
■ Providing advance information (before the briefing) by email
■ Using short videos that are concise (one to two minutes long)

- Using images/pictures
- Using storyboards
- Using mind maps, fishbone diagrams, or other illustrations that summarize a large amount of information concisely.

What Are the Roles of Team Leaders and Team Facilitators in This Phase?

The briefing phase is often the first meeting of an AAL team. It is often the "forming" stage for the team in the famous Bruce Tuckman (1965) stages of group development—that is, forming, storming, norming, and performing. During the forming stage, team members are unfamiliar with each other and are not sure what each team member can bring to the AAL team project.

During the forming stage, the team leader should take notes during the briefing provided by the manager and, after the briefing, host a team meeting to determine what skills each team member possesses that could help to deal with the issue. It is important early in the AAL set to establish which skills each team member can bring.

During the forming stage, the team facilitator should facilitate an icebreaker to help team members grow more familiar with each other. When people do not know each other, they are reluctant to interact. That natural reluctance to interact will lead to a slow start to projects—unless a team facilitator can break the ice faster and set team members at their ease.

One person may play the role of team leader and team facilitator. On those occasions, the team leader should use questioning to draw out the team members. Questions will prompt team members to think and to listen to each struggle to answer those questions. When the focus of the team effort is turned to answering questions, it helps to set people at ease and get them to apply creative thinking about ways to address the issue confronting the team.

How is Reflection Used in This Phase?

A good briefing will do more than merely provide information. It should prompt curiosity, build worker engagement and motivation to address the issue, and inspire early efforts to think of ways to solve the problem, meet the training challenge, formulate or implement a vision, or achieve a goal. The briefing should provide a foundation for a more thorough investigation to provide missing details.

There is more than one way to organize a briefing. One approach is, in less than an hour, to:

- Open with a description of the business problem, training challenge, vision, or goal (that is, the issues) by answering the journalistic questions of who is affected, what is happening, when did the issue grow in importance, where is the issue important, how did the issue appear, and how much might it cost the organization?
- Provide known facts about the issue(s) (that is, give the backstory and background)
- Explain why the problem, training challenge, vision, or goal is important to the organization (answer the questions "So what?," "Who cares?" and "Why is this issue important?")
- Provide a short anecdote that illustrates why the AAL team members should care about the issue (appeal to their heart/emotion by showing how this issue might affect the people on the AAL team, if that is possible)
- Describe why the AAL team was formed
- Introduce the AAL team members and explain why each member was chosen (what skills they bring to the project and what development needs for individuals are to be addressed)
- Introduce the team leader and team facilitator if they have already been identified (some AAL teams will vote to appoint their own team leaders or team facilitators)
- Open the briefing to questions and answers from those present.

Reflection can be prompted after each step in the briefing process. That can be accomplished by posing open questions that will encourage those participating in the briefing to think about each part of the briefing. Review Exhibit 4.2 to see how reflection might be prompted in each stage of a briefing.

Exhibit 4.2 The Role of Reflection in a Briefing

For each step in an organizational scheme for a briefing shown in the left-hand column below, note the role that could be played to prompt reflection in that step in the right-hand column.

	Organizational Scheme for a Briefing	How to Prompt Reflection in This Step of the Briefing
1	Open with a description of the business problem, training challenge, vision, or goal (that is, the issues) by answering the journalistic questions of who is affected, what is happening, when did the issue grow in importance, where is the issue of importance, how did the issue appear, and how much might it be costing the organization?	• What have you (participants in the briefing) heard about this problem, training challenge, vision, or goal? • Who do you think is affected? • Do you have any idea what is happening? • When do you think this problem grew in importance, assuming that you think it did? • Where is the issue especially prominent or important in the organization? • How much might this issue be costing the organization?
2	Provide known facts about the issue(s) (that is, give the backstory and background)	• What do we know for sure about this issue? • What do you already know about this issue, and how do you know it?
3	Explain why the problem, training challenge, vision, or goal is of importance to the organization (answer the questions "So what?", "Who cares?" and "Why is this issue important?")	• Why is this issue of importance to the organization? • How do we answer the question "So what?" • Who cares about this problem, and why do they care? • Why is this issue of importance to anyone?
4	Provide, if possible, a short anecdote that illustrates why the AAL team members should care about the issue (appeal to their heart/emotion by showing how this issue might affect the people on the AAL team, if that is possible)	• Has anyone on the AAL team heard a story about this issue? If so, what is the story? • What is the meaning of the story?
5	Describe why the AAL team was formed	• What is an AAL team, and why is it useful? • What model describes an AAL team?

6	Introduce the AAL team members and explain why each member was chosen (what skills they bring to the project and what development needs they need to address)	• Who is serving on the AAL team? • Why was each member chosen? • Does each member, once he/she hears the reason he/she was chosen for the team, agree with the reason(s) he/she was chosen? • What does each member stand to learn by participating in this AAL team?
7	Introduce the team leader and team facilitator if they are already known (some AAL teams will vote to appoint their own team leaders or team facilitators)	• Who is the team leader? • Why was he/she chosen to be team leader? • Who is the team facilitator? • Why was he/she chosen to be the team facilitator?
8	Open the briefing to questions and answers from those present	• What questions do you have at the end of the briefing? • Who can take notes during the question-and-answer session so that AAL team members may remember, and reflect on, these questions for possible future investigations?

Emphasize that briefings should be free of unsupported opinions or editorializing. The individual(s) delivering the briefing—whether a manager or an AAL team member—should refrain from any discussion that biases the views of the AAL team. Editorializing during a briefing will bias outcomes, and that will not prompt creative solutions or generate breakthrough results.

It may also be wise to videotape or record the briefing so that AAL team members may refer to it again, as they may need to do so. Human memory is faulty. People forget about 80 percent of what they hear within 48 hours. If a video recording of the briefing can help AAL team members recall critical issues, then it is worth doing.

What Should Be Considered for Virtual and Hybrid Settings in This Phase?

Not all briefings will occur face to face. Onsite briefings are rare if the organization is geographically dispersed and if AAL team members are (in part) chosen for geographical representation. Even if team members work in the same facility, they may still opt to participate due to the complexity of traveling from one part of the company to other parts. (If you do not know what I mean, try moving from one US government building to another. You will quickly find such tough security that it will be easier to meet in a Starbucks than to try to travel from one government building to another. The same principle may also apply in some businesses.)

How Can This Phase Be Evaluated?

A briefing can be evaluated much like a training program. Consider for evaluation such issues as these:

■ Did the briefing provide sufficient information for the AAL team about the issue (problem, vision, training challenge, or goal)?
■ Was the briefing concise, and was time during the briefing used wisely?
■ How much information was provided in the briefing on target for the issue and relevant to the AAL team?
■ How much did the briefing prompt creative thinking that could lead to innovative solutions?
■ How well did the briefing prompt reflection?
■ How well did the briefing help to develop AAL team members in line with their individual and collective development needs?

Other evaluative questions could be posed—depending on what managers want to know about and what AAL team members may want to consider.

Avoiding the Most Common Mistakes

Like any other phase in accelerated action learning, the briefing phase is subject to several common mistakes. Among those are the following:

■ The briefing might be delayed after the team is organized and assembled, leaving team members confused about what to do and when to start
■ The briefing might be biased, with managers (or AAL team members) giving their opinions confronting the AAL team and how to address

those (such as the causes of problems, the nature of a training challenge, the shape of a vision to be formulated, or methods of achieving goals)

■ The briefing might be delivered by a manager who has gathered no information before the briefing, leaving the AAL team confused about what they are to do and why. (That can happen when the manager's immediate supervisor wants to commission the AAL team but delegates responsibility for doing the briefing. It is a tactic that will probably mislead an AAL team)

■ The briefing might be incomplete, leaving it up to AAL team members to gather necessary facts before the team can begin formulating solutions to problems, training design to deal with a training challenge, an initial vision, or clarity on the goal to be achieved

References

Hollins, P. (2022). *Build rapid expertise: How to learn faster, acquire knowledge more thoroughly, comprehend deeper, and reach a world-class level* (3rd ed). Independently Published.

Tuckman, B. W. (1965). Developmental sequence in small groups. *Psychological Bulletin, 63*(6), 384–399.

Exhibit 4.3 A Tool for Organizing an Accelerated Action Learning Briefing

Directions: Use this tool to organize your thinking for making a briefing to an AAL team about a business problem, a training challenge, a vision to be formulated or realized, or a business goal to be achieved. For each action step appearing in the left-hand column below, write notes for the briefing in the right-hand column. When you finish, you should have the basis for a well-organized briefing.	
Action Steps	**Your Notes for the Briefing**
1 Describe the problem, training challenge, vision, or goal to be achieved	
2 Provide facts about the issue to be addressed by the AAL team	

3	Explain why the problem, training challenge, vision, or goal is of importance to the organization	
4	Provide, if possible, a short anecdote that illustrates why the AAL team members should care about the issue	
5	Describe why the AAL team was formed	
6	Introduce the AAL team members and explain why each member was chosen	
7	Introduce the team leader and team facilitator, if they are already known	
8	Open the briefing to questions and answers from those present	
9	Add any other information of relevance to the briefing	

Chapter 5

Phase 4: Establishing Measurable Goals for the Action Learning Set

What is the fourth phase of the accelerated action learning model (AALM)? The fourth phase is to establish measurable goals for the action learning set (see Exhibit 5.1). Measurable goals are typically established for the results desired (that is, the outputs sought from the AAL team's work). Think of AAL goals as being akin to the objectives sought from a training program. Instructional objectives in training state what learners should know, do, or feel upon completion of the training program. Performance objectives in training state what learners should know, do, or feel about their jobs after the training is completed. Measurable goals for an AAL team state the results sought from the AAL work.

This chapter opens with a case story about establishing measurable goals for an AAL team. The chapter also examines how measurable goals for an AAL team can be established, the role that microlearning can play in this phase, and reviews the roles that team leaders and team facilitators can play in this fourth phase. The chapter also examines how individual reflection plays a part in this phase, delineates how virtual and hybrid settings should be considered in this phase, lists common mistakes made in this phase, and offers tips on how to solve, or avoid, those common mistakes. The chapter ends with a tool suitable for on-the-job application, and that tool provides practical help in establishing measurable goals.

 DOI: 10.4324/9781003348658-5

The Accelerated Action Learning Model (AALM)

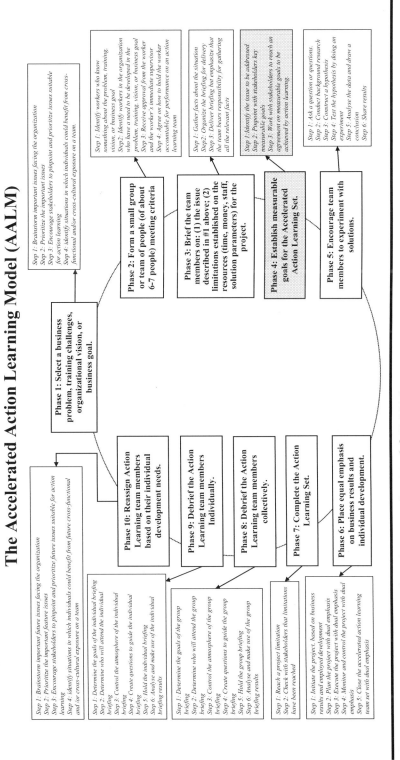

Step 1: Brainstorm important issues facing the organization
Step 2: Prioritize the important issues
Step 3: Encourage stakeholders to pinpoint and prioritize issues suitable for action learning
Step 4: Identify situations in which individuals could benefit from cross-functional and/or cross-cultural exposure on a team.

Step 1: Identify workers who know something about the problem, training, vision, or business goal
Step 2: Identify workers in the organization who have a need to be developed in the problem, training, vision, or business goal
Step 3: Receive approval from the worker and the worker's immediate supervisor
Step 4: Agree on how to hold the worker accountable for performance on an action learning team

Step 1: Gather facts about the situation
Step 2: Organize the briefing for delivery
Step 3: Deliver briefing but emphasize that the team bears responsibility for gathering all the relevant facts

Step 1: Identify the issue to be addressed
Step 2: Pinpoint with stakeholders key measurable goals
Step 3: Work with stakeholders to reach an agreement on measurable goals to be achieved by action learning.

Step 1: Ask a question or questions.
Step 2: Conduct background research
Step 3: Construct a hypothesis
Step 4: Test the hypothesis by doing an experiment
Step 5: Analyse the data and draw a conclusion
Step 6: Share results

Phase 1: Select a business problem, training challenges, organizational vision, or business goal.

Phase 2: Form a small group or team of people (of about 6-7 people) meeting criteria

Phase 3: Brief the team members on: (1) the issue described in #1 above; (2) limitations established on the resources (time, money, staff, solution parameters) for the project.

Phase 4: Establish measurable goals for the Accelerated Action Learning Set.

Phase 5: Encourage team members to experiment with solutions.

Phase 10: Reassign Action Learning team members based on their individual development needs.

Phase 9: Debrief the Action Learning team members Individually.

Phase 8: Debrief the Action Learning team members collectively.

Phase 7: Complete the Action Learning Set.

Phase 6: Place equal emphasis on business results and individual development.

Step 1: Brainstorm important future issues facing the organization
Step 2: Prioritize the important feature issues
Step 3: Encourage stakeholders to pinpoint and prioritize future issues suitable for action learning
Step 4: Identify situations in which individuals could benefit from future cross-functional and /or cross-cultural exposure on a team

Step 1: Determine the goals of the individual briefing
Step 2: Determine who will attend the individual briefing
Step 3: Control the atmosphere of the individual briefing
Step 4: Create questions to guide the individual briefing
Step 5: Hold the individual briefing
Step 6: Analyse and make use of the individual briefing results

Step 1: Determine the goals of the group briefing
Step 2: Determine who will attend the group briefing
Step 3: Control the atmosphere of the group briefing
Step 4: Create questions to guide the group briefing
Step 5: Hold the group briefing
Step 6: Analyse and make use of the group briefing results

Step 1: Reach a project limitation
Step 2: Check with stakeholders that limitations have been reached

Step 1: Initiate the project, based on business results and employed development
Step 2: Plan the project with dual emphasis
Step 3: Execute the project with dual emphasis
Step 4: Monitor and control the project with dual emphasis
Step 5: Close the accelerated action learning team set with dual emphasis

Exhibit 5.1   The Accelerated Action Learning Model (AALM)

Opening Case Story

Jennifer Morgan is a front-line supervisor of staff assistants at a Big Ten university. She works in one department of that university. She oversees a group of ten staff assistants.

Recently, the department has had problems in attracting undergraduate and graduate enrollments and keeping students that enroll. It is not a problem unusual to higher education institutes in the US. Many universities face precipitous drops in enrollments and significant dropout rates of existing students.

Jennifer asks the Department Head if she can form an AAL team to explore what the department can do to increase enrollments and build sustainable enrollment. The Department Head agrees but insists that Jennifer should create a team that includes representation by (at least) faculty, staff assistants, undergraduate students, and graduate students.

Jennifer assembles the AAL team. After giving the team a briefing (at which the Department Head attended and offered words of staunch support) in which the trends in enrollment and dropout rates were shown on graphs, Jennifer asked the team how they should measure the success of the AAL team. What targets (measures) should they establish for success? When they completed their work and their pilot tests of creative approaches to solving the enrollment problems, what kind of measurable results should have been achieved? Answering that question touched off a debate that lasted over several meetings. Eventually, the team agreed upon measurable goals: a 10 percent increase in enrollments and a 10 percent reduction in dropout rates.

What Are the Steps in Establishing Measurable Goals for an Accelerated Action Learning Group on an Issue?

Step 1: Identify the Issue to be Addressed

The first step in this phase is to identify exactly what is the issue (or issues) to be addressed by the AAL team project.

That step would normally be described by the team sponsor(s) during the team briefing. However, team sponsors may have:

- Confused symptoms with root causes
- Misdiagnosed the problem to be solved

- Incomplete or faulty information about the problem to be solved, the training challenge to be met, the vision to be formulated or implemented, or the goal to be achieved.

It is important for the AAL team—led by the Team Leader and helped by the Team Facilitator—to take nothing for granted. They should regard the information delivered during the initial AAL team briefing with healthy skepticism. The AAL team should launch its own investigation of what issues need to be addressed by the AAL set.

Step 2: Pinpoint Stakeholders' Key Measurable Goals

Stakeholders are those who stand to be affected by the results of the AAL set. Stakeholders may include:

- Team sponsors (whose budget might subsidize the team project)
- Managers
- Workers
- Unions and union leaders
- Those outside the organization (such as family members of employees or members of the community surrounding the business) who might be affected by the organization's actions
- Members of the AAL team (they can also be important stakeholders because they must support the metrics chosen and be willing to defend them when others attack or criticize the measures that the team chose).

The important questions are (1) who are the most important stakeholders for the AAL team set and (2) what metrics matter most to them?

If there are multiple stakeholders for AAL—and there often are—then it may be necessary to collaborate with representatives of each stakeholder group to clarify what metrics might be of most importance to them. Financial measures, which are often emphasized in the human resources field (and expressed as a desire for return-on-investment measures), might primarily interest only some of the key stakeholder groups. Other groups may care more about issues other than financial measures.

Step 3: Work with Stakeholders to Reach Agreement on Measurable Goals to be Achieved by Action Learning

Once the information has been collected from different stakeholder groups about what measurable goals are of primary importance to each group, then the AAL team can finalize the measurable goals the team will use.

Note that it is possible to change the metrics during an AAL set. Why is that? Simple: when an AAL team undertakes a project, the team members are entering at the base of a learning curve. As the team gains experience with the issue, the team progresses up the learning curve. That means the team has more information by which to make good decisions. As the team gains experience, the team members may realize that the metrics chosen are not the best, not appropriate, not complete, or need to be supplemented with other metrics (*"Learning curves in project management,"* 2020).

What Role Does Microlearning Play in This Phase?

Few people are experts on measurement and metrics. Establishing measurable goals for an AAL team can be challenging.

There are two ways microlearning can play a role in this phase.

The first way is that the AAL team members will need some general information or even training on measurement and metrics—particularly as it applies to human resource issues. In the HR field, measurement and metrics are sometimes called *HR analytics* (for example Burkholder et al., 2007; Ferrar and Green, 2021; Fitz-Enz, 2009; Fitz-Enz and Davison, 2006; Walsh, 2021).

Such general information is easily available online—either on websites on the topic or as videos about how to measure and what metrics can be used in HR (see, for instance, *"Introduction to metrics,"* 2021; *"Introduction to metrics,"* n.d.). Typical topics, when introducing metrics, are to discuss what metrics and measurements are; what kinds of metrics exist; how to establish metrics; how to gain agreement on using metrics; how to present metrics (such as scorecards, dashboards, and so forth); how to change metrics; and the behavioral impact on people of measuring ("what gets measured gets done").

The second way is that AAL team members may need information (and thus some microlearning experiences) about how the organization measures performance in the challenge (that is, the problem under investigation, the vision being formulated or implemented, the training challenge to be addressed, or the goal to be achieved) and benchmarking information, if available, on how other organizations measure the challenge. That may require investigation to address such questions as: (1) how has the issue (problem, vision, training, or goal) been measured? (2) what are stakeholder/management preferences on how the issue should be measured? (3) what are desired measurable targets to be achieved, based on the opinions of key stakeholders and AAL team members, as well as results of research on common business practices and global best practices, if the latter information is available?

It should be emphasized that microlearning must be organized according to bite-sized chunks of learning. Using it will not help to create lengthy training programs or complicated job aids; instead, the information must be presented in ways that can be quickly absorbed and used by AAL team members as they investigate the issue(s) and/or experiment with possible actions to address the issue(s). Recall that typical approaches to microlearning include infographics, short text descriptions (one half-page or less), explainer videos, animated descriptions, brief games, short phone apps, and others. For more information on microlearning, check out sources like Kapp and DeFelice (2019).

What Are the Roles of Team Leaders and Team Facilitators in This Phase?

The team leader and the team facilitator must take active roles in this phase.

The team leader must be sure that the AAL team members have been given adequate background information on measurements and metrics relevant to the issue confronting the team. That includes ways to establish and set up a project plan to guide the actions of the AAL team. Typically, that would include setting up action steps (and measures/metrics associated with those), timelines for progressing through the action steps, before/after measures of pilot test experiments undertaken by the AAL team to try out solutions to the issues, budget tracking metrics relevant to the AAL project, and success measures for experiments. Metrics must be captured for experiments with solutions, visions, training, or goals to show AAL sponsors what progress has been made by the AAL team. Those metrics must also be presented in visually appealing ways—such as dashboards. The team leader is typically responsible for making the final decisions on the team about what measures will be used and how they will be presented.

The team facilitator's role in this phase is to ensure that team members learn about measurements and metrics. Given the importance of measures in today's business world, it is a critical issue to ensure that workers (and managers) have mastered them. The team facilitator should ensure that the team leader does not make unilateral decisions about what measures to use or how to conduct measurement; rather, the team leader should involve (and, when necessary, educate) team members about options in measurement.

How Is Reflection Used in This Phase?

Reflection is critical in the fourth phase of accelerated action learning. Measurement can be harmful if conducted without mindful reflection on the implications of the measures chosen (Muller, 2018; Yushenko, 2018).

As an AAL team is briefed on the application of measurements and metrics in meeting the challenge posed by the AAL set, the team facilitator should normally take the lead in posing tough, challenging questions to stimulate reflection.

For instance, as the AAL team is briefed on what metrics and measurements are, the team facilitator may pose such questions as these:

■ What might be the downside of using measurements and metrics for this issue?
■ Who might want measures the most, and what will they do with the metrics we give them?
■ What metrics might be most useful to the AAL team to track progress?
■ What is the best time to collect measures, and how will the team know the time is right?

As the AAL team investigates common business practices and global best practices in measuring the issue, the team facilitator may pose such questions as these:

■ What is compelling about the measures and metrics typically used to assess this issue?
■ What might be missing or faulty about the measures and metrics typically used to assess this issue?

■ Why do you (the AAL team) suppose these measures/metrics are chosen?

As the AAL team considers adopting measures and metrics by which to assess pilot tests or experiments to solve a problem, meet a training challenge, formulate or implement a vision or achieve a goal, the team facilitator might pose such questions as:

■ Will these measures/metrics assess what is important?
■ How will decision-makers use these measures/metrics?
■ Are there any unexpected side effects that might result from using these measurements or metrics?
■ What change has occurred between measures captured before corrective action (like the experiment) was undertaken and those captured after the corrective action?
■ Did the action taken by the AAL team identify the driver or reason for any change in measures, or is it possible that confounding variables may have affected measures? If so, how?

There may be other issues worthy of exploration when examining measurements and metrics. One of those is to determine what weight to place on so-called financial measures (such as return on investment or cost/benefit analysis) and what weight to place on so-called non-financial measures (such as changes in measures of customer satisfaction, market penetration, efficiency measures of business operations, learning and growth measures of workers, or social changes in the community).

What Should Be Considered for Virtual and Hybrid Settings in This Phase?

The venue for establishing measurable goals for an accelerated action learning set should make only a slight difference in the ultimate results of this phase. But maybe AAL team actions may be accelerated—that is, made to move more efficiently and effectively—by using virtual methods. The reasons for that should be simple.

First, giving team members background briefings on how to measure and what metrics might be used can be conducted by individual team members and then posted to spreadsheets or assembled in central collaborative work-spaces like Google Docs. Using virtual methods may move faster than wait-ing for face-to-face meetings.

Second, when team members are geographically scattered around the globe, arranging face-to-face virtual meetings may be a challenge due to differences in time zones. However, posting information to spreadsheets or other decision-support software can make sharing information more efficient and effective.

Team discussions held to generate creative ideas should be conducted online. About 56 percent of workers report they are more creative when working online than when they are working onsite (Eatough, 2021; Tskipurski, 2021). The level of communication among AAL team members may be affected when the team works remotely, and that may call for new skills from the team facilitator to improve virtual interpersonal communica-tion (Rothwell and Park, 2021; Teledataict, 2017). Communication is influ-enced when people discourse online. Consider that studies show that less than 10 percent of communication is based on the written or verbal word, the other 90 percent being based on non-verbal body language. As much as 40 to 50 percent of online communication can lead to misunderstandings or miscommunication because so much is left out without body language or non-verbal communication to help carry the message. However, much software exists to facilitate collaboration and communication online (Duffy, 2023), and using it can enhance AAL team efficiency and effectiveness.

How Can This Phase Be Evaluated?

The best way to evaluate this phase is to involve an array of different stake-holders in weighing up the relative value of the measurements and metrics used in this phase. For example, as AAL team members consider which measurements/metrics to capture before implementing their pilot tests or experiments, do those measures satisfy team sponsors and are the metrics on target for evaluating what is important?

A simple example will illustrate. Imagine that the AAL team is tasked to investigate ways to reduce avoidable turnover. Turnover is a consequence of other cause(s) and is not a problem to be solved. (What leads to the turnover is the root cause.) Before undertaking an experiment to reduce turnover, an AAL team should capture a baseline of turnover before any experiment is undertaken. Then, as a pilot test or an experiment is mounted to reduce turnover, the AAL team can track what changes result from the corrective action the team has undertaken. But, in this example, it would be unwise to assume that measurements identified by the AAL team alone would be adequate to satisfy team sponsors. The team sponsors should be consulted on what metrics to measure.

It is also possible to evaluate the key issues to be addressed by the AAL team. That means some ways should be established to evaluate what business problems the AAL team solved because of participation in the accelerated action learning set, and what skills the AAL team members acquired or enhanced individually and collectively during the AAL set. One way to measure that is to ask the team members what skills they acquired as a group and individually; another way to measure is to ask the team members what business problems they believe they solved.

Avoiding the Most Common Mistakes

Several mistakes are common when establishing measures or metrics in an AAL set.

The most common mistake is to avoid creating any metrics or measures. That can happen because team sponsors and AAL team members are eager to take corrective action and find solutions to problems, formulate, or implement a vision, meet a training challenge, or achieve a business goal. The sense of urgency that impels action can trump the reasoned, thoughtful consideration of how to establish metrics that will measure what results are sought from the AAL team effort.

A second common mistake is to choose the wrong or inadequate measures or metrics. That can happen when the team leader unilaterally decides what measures to incorporate in an AAL project plan without adequately or properly involving the team sponsors, the AAL team members, or other key stakeholders. When the wrong measures are chosen, that will usually lead to actions insufficient to meet the AAL team goals. Team sponsors will be disappointed and AAL team members may feel frustrated. That may sour future worker groups from participating in AAL sets.

A third common mistake is to fail to recognize that the metrics chosen can have unintended side effects. Those have been well documented. In a classic article on that topic, Steven Kerr (1995) pointed out many examples of where a desire to measure one thing led to the choice of inappropriate measures that led to unintended side effects. As a simple example of Kerr's point, he mentioned that there is a desire to evaluate college professors for their teaching quality. However, it is tough to measure teaching quality, and the number of academic articles published by a professor is often taken as a substitute with the assumption that good professors always publish more articles. That assumption is faulty and encourages poor teaching among professors but much publishing. The same principle can apply to AAL. If the metrics chosen for an AAL set are inadequate or inappropriate for measuring the desired outcomes, then there could be unintended side effects. To control for that, AAL team members should seek a broad array of opinions about what measures/metrics to use in their baseline assessments (the status before corrective action is taken by the AAL team) and post-action assessments (the status after an experiment by the AAL team is conducted).

References

Burkholder, N., Goals, S., & Shapiro, J. (2007). *Ultimate performance: Measuring human resources at work*. Wiley.

Duffy, J. (2023, January 11). The best online collaboration software for 2023. *PC Magazine*. https://www.pcmag.com/picks/the-best-online-collaboration-software

Eatough, E. (2021, September 21). *Employees report greater creativity working remotely*. https://www.betterup.com/blog/employees-report-greater-creativity-working-remotely

Ferrar, J., & Green, D. (2021). *Excellence in people analytics*. Kogan Page.

Fitz-Enz, J. (2009). *The ROI of human capital: Measuring the economic value of human performance*. 2nd ed. Amacom.

Fitz-Enz, J., & Davison, B. (2006). *How to measure human resources*. 3rd ed. McGraw-Hill.

Introduction to metrics. (2021). https://www2.microstrategy.com/producthelp/Current/MSTRWeb/WebHelp/Lang_1033/Content/About_metrics.htm#:~:text=Metrics%20are%20MicroStrategy%20objects%20that,are%20displayed%20on%20a%20report

Introduction to metrics. (n.d.). https://help.fullstory.com/hc/en-us/articles/360052381313-Introduction-to-Metrics

Kapp, K., & DeFelice, R. (2019). *Microlearning: Short and sweet*. Association for Talent Development.

Kerr, S. (1995). On the folly of rewarding A, but hoping for B. *Academy of Management Executive*, 9(1), 7–14.

Learning curves in project management research paper. (2020, July 4). https://ivy-panda.com/essays/learning-curves-in-project-management/

Muller, J. (2018). *The tyranny of metrics*. Princeton University Press.

Rothwell, W., & Park, C. (2021). *Virtual group coaching to improve group relationships: Process consultation reimagined.* CRC Press.

Teledataict. (2017, August 31). *The internet and interpersonal relationships.* https://www.teledataict.com/the-internet-and-interpersonal-relationships/

Tskipursky, G. (2021, October 14). *Remote work can be better for innovation than in-person meetings.* Scientific American. https://www.scientificamerican.com/article/remote-work-can-be-better-for-innovation-than-in-person-meetings/

Walsh, M. (2021). *HR analytics essentials you always wanted to know.* Vibrant Publishers.

Yushenko, M. (2018, May 29). *Mindless measurement: How metrics can waste our time and literally kill.* https://mishayurchenko.me/2018/05/29/mindless-measurement-how-metrics-can-waste-our-time-and-literally-kill-us/

Exhibit 5.2 A Tool for Establishing Measurable Goals for an Action Learning Set

Directions: Use this tool to guide your accelerated action learning (AAL) team's thinking about establishing measurable goals for an AAL set. For each question posed in the left-hand column below, record the AAL team's answers in the right-hand column. It is entirely possible that the AAL team may need to do further investigations before answering all the questions, and that is actually desirable. When the tool is completed, the AAL team should have established measurable goals for the accelerated action learning set.

	Questions	Answers
1	Who are the accelerated action learning (AAL) team's sponsor(s), and how do they measure the issue that is the focus of the AAL team's investigation? (The issue might include a business problem to be solved, a training challenge to be met, a vision to be formulated or implemented, or a goal to be achieved by the AAL team.)	
2	What measures or metrics are commonly used by other organizations to address the issue? What measures or metrics are used by global best practice organizations?	

3	When are metrics typically measured? Is it common to capture a baseline before corrective action is taken and then also measure after the action is taken? If so, what are the metrics used, if known?	
4	Where are the metrics measured? Are there any cross-cultural differences? (For instance, are the same measures used in all countries or at all company facilities?)	
5	Why are metrics gathered? What decisions are made based on the metrics?	
6	How are measures/metrics gathered?	
7	How are measures/metrics presented? (Are there common dashboards or other visually appealing ways of depicting the metrics?)	
8	How are the measure/metrics communicated to workers and managers?	
9	What unintended side effects might result from using the most common measures/metrics, and how can their side effects be minimized or avoided?	
10	What metrics or measures are most appropriate for this AAL set, and why are they appropriate?	

Chapter 6

Phase 5: Encouraging Team Members to Experiment with Solutions

What is the fifth phase of the accelerated action learning model (AALM)? The fifth phase is the point where team members experiment with solutions to business problems, design, develop and implement a training effort, formulate, and implement a vision, or work to achieve a business goal (see Exhibit 6.1). Experiments attempt to address the issue that prompted the need for the AAL team's work. Think of this step as consisting of one or more pilot tests. It is an application of rapid prototyping. It can be the heart of the accelerated action learning (AAL) experience.

This chapter opens with a case story about a team experimenting with solutions. The chapter also examines how experiments can be designed, the role that microlearning can play in this phase, and reviews the roles that team leaders and team facilitators can play in this fifth phase. The chapter also examines how individual reflection plays a part in this phase, delineates how virtual and hybrid settings should be considered in this phase, lists common mistakes made in this phase, and offers tips on how to solve, or avoid, those common mistakes. The chapter ends with a tool suitable for guiding experiments.

Note at the outset of this chapter that although the design of experiments (DOE) can be used in AAL, it is not essential. *The design of experiments (DOE) is a field of applied statistics concerned with the planning, execution, analysis, and interpretation of controlled tests to analyze the factors*

The Accelerated Action Learning Model (AALM)

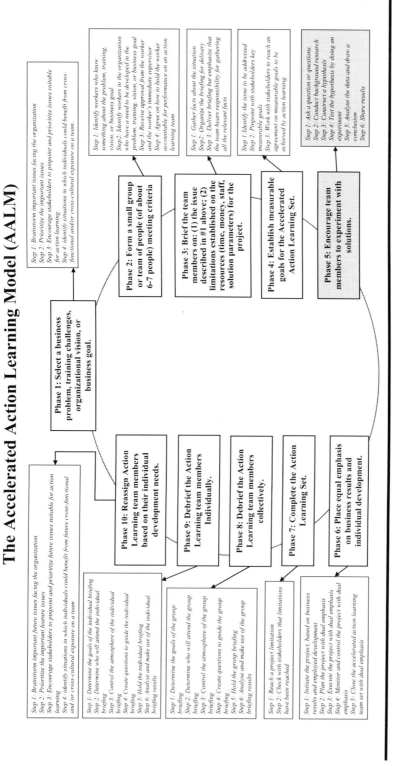

Exhibit 6.1   The Accelerated Action Learning Model (AALM)

that exert influence ("*What is the design of experiments?*" n.d.). DOE is a versatile data gathering and analysis method that may be applied to many experiments.

More relevant to the experiment phase is design thinking. *Design thinking* is a non-linear, iterative process that focuses on cooperation between designers and users. It brings to life creative ideas based on what real users think, feel, and do. A human-centered design approach often focuses on five fundamental stages: empathize, define, ideate, prototype, and test.

Opening Case Story

Fenton Smith has been appointed as a team leader for an AAL experience. Along with his colleague Loretta Morgan, who serves as the team's facilitator, Fenton's AAL team is tasked to explore new insurance products. Fenton, who is a certified project manager, and Loretta, who is a certified facilitator, work with five additional team members who come from different departments and various levels of the organization chart from the Vigilant Insurance Company. The team members are well qualified: the team has a supervisor from the underwriting department; an actuary; a manager from the service-after-the-sale department (customer service); a manager from human resources; and a writer from the company's communications department.

The AAL team faces many questions. They must consider:

■ How many ideas for new insurance products can they produce in the time they have? (three months)
■ What are the preferences of key stakeholders for new insurance products?
■ What is the insurance market like, and how might that influence decisions about new products?
■ What have been the trends in new insurance products? Are there identifiable patterns in new insurance products?
■ Who are the customers?

Fenton and Loretta have been meeting with the team, and the team members have divided up the questions among themselves to investigate. The team realizes that the questions must be answered quickly before the team can get to experiment with possible new insurance products. That must be done within the three months the team has been given to carry out their AAL project.

What Are the Steps to Guide Team Experimentation?

There are at least six steps in this phase. They will be examined in this chapter section. They are: (1) ask a question or questions; (2) conduct background research; (3) construct a hypothesis (or series of research questions/objectives); (4) test the hypotheses or else answer the research questions/objectives by doing one or more experiments; (5) analyze the data and draw a conclusion; and (6) share results with AAL team members, AAL team sponsors, and other stakeholders.

Step 1: Ask a Question or Questions

Once the briefing is completed in Phase 3 and the measurable goals are established in Phase 4, it is time for the AAL team to assemble and begin brainstorming on the task confronting them—such as solving a business problem, meeting a training challenge, formulating or implementing a company vision, or achieving a business goal.

Typically, at this point, the AAL team will enter the "storming" stage of small-group development. At that stage, team members ask many questions. Among them:

- Is this assignment/team project even necessary?
- Who assigned this project, and what is his/her/their agenda?
- Who cares about this project, and why is it important?
- When does the team begin its work, and how long will be given for it?
- How does this team project factor into individual key performance indicators for the jobs?
- Will this team project be full time or part time? Will it be done onsite, online, or by hybrid means?

In the "storming" stage, the team comes to grips with the issue and internalizes that issue by struggling to understand what it is, who cares about it, how it affects them and their business, and how they can move forward as a team.

After the storming stage is completed, or even as part of that stage, AAL team members will ask many questions about the issue confronting the team and ways of solving the business problem, meeting the training challenge, formulating or implementing the vision, or achieving the business goal. Often, there will be matters to be investigated, first after the initial briefing. Questions must be posed about what information is lacking before the team can tackle the project. Then, additional investigation may lead to questions about ways to address the issue confronting the AAL team.

Step 2: Conduct Background Research

After the briefing, the AAL team should brainstorm what additional information is needed. That will require background research about the issue confronting the team. Once that background information is gathered, the AAL team must decide how to use that information to construct a hypothesis about ways to address the issue.

Step 3: Construct an Hypothesis

It is possible to state formal research hypotheses to be tested by the AAL team in its efforts to meet the team challenge. It is also possible to state less formal research questions or state objectives to guide the team effort.

The AAL team may need to be briefed on how to state hypotheses, if that approach is used, or else how to construct research questions or research objectives. The AAL team may need a formal briefing on those topics (Allen, 2016; Enago Academy, 2023; McCombes, 2023; *"Research objectives,"* n.d.).

Step 4: Test the Hypothesis by Doing an Experiment

During the experimentation step, the AAL team tries out ways to solve the business problem(s), meet the training needs, formulate or implement a business vision, or achieve a business goal. Often, the AAL team will try out many ways of finding an answer to the issue they have been confronted with. That may require rapid prototyping—that is, trying out many approaches to solving the problem or otherwise addressing the AAL team issue.

Step 5: Analyze the Data and Draw a Conclusion

As each experiment is completed, the team members come together to discuss what they learned from the experience and how close they have gotten to solving the problem or otherwise addressing the issue. They analyze relevant information collected during the pilot and draw conclusions about the approach they used in each experiment.

Often many experiments are performed to find an answer.

Step 6: Share Results

The last step in this phase is to share results of each experiment with the AAL team sponsors and with other relevant stakeholders. That can be done through:

- Regular action reports (To answer the question "What have we done lately?")
- Regular, periodic briefings (like weekly, biweekly, monthly, or even quarterly briefings)
- Meetings between the AAL team and others (such as AAL team sponsors and other key stakeholders).

During the experiments, AAL team members may be actively involved with groups participating in the experiments and giving the members feedback on what is happening with the experiment. For instance, if an innovative approach to greeting customers is tried out in a retail store, there may be a need to discuss regularly how that experiment is going with the retail clerks and retail managers participating in the experiments.

What Role Does Microlearning Play in This Phase?

As AAL team members produce questions and as they generate ideas for experiments, they are bound to need information. Usually, there is little time to do in-depth investigations. What AAL team members need to do is find relevant information quickly to inform their ideas about experiments to try out to solve a business problem, meet a training challenge, formulate or implement a vision, or achieve a business goal. It is where microlearning can be most aptly applied.

The finest microlearning combines video, quizzes, and visuals to create a dynamic experience. The goal is to keep it short. AAL team members often generate ideas, split them up to investigate, and then produce microlearning experiences of five minutes or less each to brief their teammates on what they find. AAL team members need not be expert trainers to design and deliver microlearning to their teammates.

Recall from earlier chapters that examples of microlearning might include (Brown, 2021):

- Short text segments (one-half page or less)
- Pictures or infographics
- Storyboards (like comic books that tell a story)
- Interactive PowerPoint slides
- Checklists
- Worksheets.

But the goals are to keep those microlearning resources *short*, *focused*, and *engaging*.

What Are the Roles of Team Leaders and Team Facilitators in This Phase?

In all except for first two phases of AAL, team leaders keep the team members on task, and the team facilitator keeps team members working together. The team leader's focus is on project management to ensure that the team completes its challenge to solve a problem, address a training challenge, formulate, or implement a vision, or achieve a goal on time and under budget. The team facilitator's role is to ensure that the team members collectively learn from the AAL team experience and work together effectively.

In this phase, and as experiments are designed and conducted, it is important to ensure that all team members are engaged. It is not helpful to have silent members or those engaged in "social loafing." It is the role of the team facilitator to ensure "all hands-on deck" and the role of the team leader to ensure that experiments are designed in efficient and effective ways, carried out promptly, and the results are communicated to team sponsors and stakeholders.

How is Reflection Used in This Phase?

Reflection is critically important in this phase of AAL. The reason is simple enough. Experimentation is carried out to explore ideas that work—and what ideas do not. Experimentation is pointless if nothing is learned from it. And essential to learning is reflecting on what might work, construct an experiment, collect the results, and then reflect on what worked in the experiment and what did not.

Each step of this phase can be the focus of reflection.

Consider: in the first step of this phase, asking questions requires reflection on what questions might lead to the best information and the best experiments. Formulating the right questions requires reflection. Typically, the team facilitator leads one or more sessions in which team members generate a list of ideas for investigation or action.

In the second step of this phase, background research requires the team facilitator to lead the team to explore necessary information about the issues and about brainstormed solutions. The team facilitator must usually lead the team in brainstorming activities to generate questions both about the background of the issue and about possible solutions or ways of addressing the issue(s). Those brainstorming activities should tap into deep reflection. Meditation exercises can help.

In the third step of this phase, the team must construct one or more hypotheses, research objectives, or research questions. Doing that may require reflection from team members working individually and collectively. Team facilitators can help guide that reflection.

In the fourth step of this phase, AAL team members conduct one or more experiments to try out ways of addressing the issues confronting the AAL team. Reflection is important in each experiment to guide future issues worthy of additional exploration and experimentation. Team facilitators often have an important role to play in prompting reflection from individual team members and in group meetings with all team members.

In the fifth step of this phase, AAL team members analyze the data. Although that may be a first step, the data lead to evidence-based conclusions. Team members must reflect on what they discovered from the experiment(s) to prompt future experiments that may be needed.

Finally, in the sixth and final step of this phase, AAL team members must share results with interested groups, such as AAL team sponsors and other stakeholders. As feedback is given to those groups, the groups may pose questions about progress on experiments that may spawn additional reflection and insights from the AAL team.

What Should Be Considered for Virtual and Hybrid Settings in This Phase?

In this phase it should not matter much if AAL teams work onsite, online, or in a hybrid format. Team members can usually divide up the work after an initial team meeting and carry out their tasks individually. But there are advantages that can be gained when team members are onsite and can develop an *esprit de corps* and camaraderie in confronting the tasks they face.

How Can This Phase Be Evaluated?

There are two ways to conceptualize evaluation during the experiment phase.

The first way to think of evaluation is that the AAL team experience can be the focus. The AAL team members may be regularly questioned about how well the team members feel that the team is addressing the business issue confronting it. They may also be polled regularly about how much they are working together harmoniously and learning, individually or collectively, during the AAL team project. The team facilitator often takes the lead in addressing these issues.

The second way to think of evaluation is that the AAL challenge—the business problem to be solved or other issue—can be the focus of attention. When each experiment ends, the AAL team may be tasked to consider how well the experiment addressed the issue. How well was the problem solved during the experiment? How well was the training need addressed by the team?

How well was the vision formulated or implemented? How well was the business goal achieved? Often these questions may have to be posed at the end of each experiment, and the team leader will spearhead efforts to discover the answers to the questions.

Avoiding the Most Common Mistakes

Several mistakes are common during the experimentation phase.

The first common mistake is that insufficient ideas are generated to guide experiments. If team members fall into groupthink, they may go along to get along. That will not prompt innovative ideas. It is a problem that team facilitators must watch out for and try to avoid. One good way to avoid this problem is if team facilitators play the role of "devil's advocate" by questioning team members and the team leader about why they approach an issue in a certain way. Playing devil's advocate will test how committed the team members are to their plans or actions.

The second common mistake is that the wrong ideas are generated to guide experiments. That is a tough problem to avoid. If the AAL team lacks the collective skills to attack an issue, then the team may need to call in outside help to assist. But recognizing the need for that can lead to wasted time and effort.

The third common mistake is that the wrong people are involved in experiments. If, for example, the AAL team asks managers to volunteer some people to participate in experiments, the wrong people might be involved. If that happens, the results of experiments may wind up wrong or misleading. It is important for the team leader to take responsibility for clarifying exactly what profile should be established for participation in experiments. Clear communication about who should be volunteered can help avoid this problem.

The fourth common mistake is that the results of the experiments are not properly captured. If the experiment is conducted but data are not recorded—or baseline data before the experiment are not established—the experiment might prove to be a waste of time because no information is captured about what happened during the experiment. There is nothing more maddening than launching into an experiment only to discover at the end nobody was taking notes or recording critical data. It is the team leader's job to ensure that that mistake is avoided.

The fifth common mistake is that experiment results are not fed back to the team sponsors or important stakeholders. If team leaders forget to record experiment results and feed those back to the people who care about them, then it will look like the AAL team is not performing properly. To avoid that problem, it is important to establish clear responsibility charts to ensure that the data are fed back in a timely and effective way (*"Responsibility charting,"* n.d.).

References

Allen, K. (2016). *Research and the analyses of research hypotheses.* Rpt. Ed. XLIBRIS.

Brown, D. (2021, October 31). *Twenty microlearning examples.* https://www.edapp .com/blog/10-microlearning-examples/

Enago Academy. (2023, January 6). *How to develop a good research hypothesis.* https://www.enago.com/academy/how-to-develop-a-good-research-hypothesis/

McCombes, S. (2023, January 30). *Writing strong research questions: Criteria & examples.* https://www.scribbr.com/research-process/research-questions/

Research objectives. (n.d.). https://www.open.edu/openlearncreate/mod/oucontent/view.php?id=231&section=8.6.2

Responsibility charting. (n.d.). https://www7.lawrence.edu/info/offices/human _resources/responsibility-charting

What is design of experiments (DOE)? (n.d.). https://asq.org/quality-resources/design -of-experiments

Exhibit 6.2 A Tool to Guide Team Experimentation

Directions: Use this Worksheet to guide your Accelerated Action Learning (AAL) team's efforts to experiment with solutions to business problems, meet training needs, formulate and/or implement business visions, and/or achieve business goals. For each step listed in the left-hand column below, write your ideas about what actions must be taken in the right-hand column. This tool can be a starting point to guide the project plan for one or more experiments to address the issue(s) confronting the AAL team.

Step in the Experimentation Phase		Your Ideas About What Actions Must Be Taken
1	Ask a question or questions	
2	Conduct background research (about the issue and about possible ways to address the issue)	
3	Construct a research hypothesis (or hypotheses), research questions, and/or research objectives (to guide experiments)	
4	Test the hypotheses or else answer the research questions/objectives by doing one or more experiments	
5	Analyze the data from the experiment(s) and draw a conclusion or conclusions	
6	Share results with AAL team members, AAL team sponsors, and other stakeholders	

Chapter 7

Phase 6: Placing Equal Emphasis on Business Results and Individual Development

What is the sixth phase of the accelerated action learning model (AALM)? The sixth phase is the point when AAL team members ensure that *equal emphasis* in the AAL team project is placed on achieving business results and developing members of the AAL team collectively and individually. This phase presents a real challenge. Most organizations regularly form work groups, teams, task forces, committees, and councils to attack problems and address business issues. But often those organizational schemes focus on the business issues first. Little or no attention is devoted to collective and individual development. It is that equal emphasis on business results and employee development that distinguishes accelerated action learning from other approaches to securing business results (see Exhibit 7.1).

This chapter opens with a case story about a team working to achieve equal emphasis on securing business results and developing the team members collectively and individually. The chapter also examines how an equal emphasis on results and employee development can be achieved, the role that microlearning can play in this phase, and reviews the roles that team leaders and team facilitators can play in this sixth phase. The chapter also examines how individual reflection plays a part in this phase, delineates how virtual and hybrid settings should be considered in this phase, lists common mistakes made in this phase, and offers tips on how to solve, or avoid, those common mistakes. The chapter ends with a tool suitable for

 DOI: 10.4324/9781003348658-7

The Accelerated Action Learning Model (AALM)

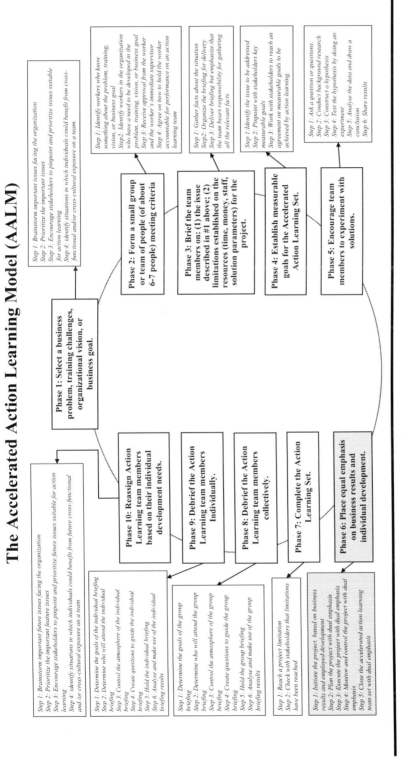

Exhibit 7.1   The Accelerated Action Learning Model (AALM)

ensuring that an equal emphasis is placed on getting business results and developing workers on the team.

Working in accelerated action learning, teams helps to build collaboration in an organization. Collaboration is critical in organizations today. Consider some statistics about collaboration cited by Boskamp (2023):

- More than half of all workers in the United States think their jobs call for collaboration.
- Approximately 75 percent of employees consider teamwork and collaboration to be vital.
- 56 percent of employers connect with employees via online collaboration tools and social media.
- 86 percent of employees in leadership positions attribute workplace failures to a lack of collaboration.
- Companies that encourage collaboration and communication at work have been related to a 50 percent reduction in employee turnover.
- Employees who collaborate at work are 17 percent more satisfied with their jobs on average.
- Workplace collaboration has increased by at least 50 percent in the past 20 years.

Unfortunately, some business leaders believe that collaboration is overdone in workplaces. For example, General Mills has reduced collaboration efforts by eight hours per week out of concern that it is growing to be too much for workers (Bakker, 2010; Cross et al., 2021). By using AAL, managers can reduce collaboration to a more controlled application, while also encouraging innovation and employee development.

Teams and other temporary organizational schemes are used in many organizations to tackle special challenges (see *"'Flash' organizations and temporary teams – On the rise?"*, 2017). Some teams consist solely of full-time workers employed by one organization. Other teams may be composed of a group representing such diverse people as contractors, subject matter experts hired from outside the organization, full-time company employees, and others. Participation by diverse groups can provide opportunities for building workers' cross-cultural competence and cross-functional competence, and to generate innovation by bringing together people with diverse viewpoints.

Opening Case Story

The Discovery Organization, Inc. assembled a cross-functional, cross-cultural team consisting of five people to identify ways for cross-functional and cross-cultural groups in the organization to work together more effectively. This AAL team was broadly diverse, representing one person from the US, one person from Europe, one person from the Middle East, one person from Asia-Pacific, and one person from Latin America. The team members also represented a relatively gender-diverse group (three women and two men) and different generational representations (one Baby Boomer, one Gen Xer, two Millennials, and one Generation Z). The five members also represented different departments in the organization and at different levels on the organization chart. (The company has a tall organization chart.)

The team members generated a list of ways to improve the functioning of diverse groups in the organization. They defined "improve" to mean that the workgroup members would be more productive while also interacting more effectively on an interpersonal level. That prompted them to research competencies on cross-functional work and for cross-cultural work. The team also prepared a draft of an assessment instrument for evaluating individuals and a training outline to encourage instruction on how diverse groups could be made more effective.

The AAL team sponsor was pleased with the outputs of the group. But, as the team was prepared to disband because the AAL team's goals had been achieved, the Team Facilitator led a discussion with all team members to ask them if they believed that equal emphasis had been placed during the AAL project on achieving business results and on collective and individual development. Once that issue was addressed with the group in a meeting, the Team Facilitator followed up with individual interviews with team members with the same questions. The result: the team members confirmed that the AAL team project had successfully met both the business goals established for the team as well as developing the team collectively and individually. Team members cited several personal examples of how they had applied what they had learned from the AAL team to their jobs.

What Are the Steps to Ensure Equal Emphasis Is Placed on Business Results and Employee Development?

Step 1: Initiate the Project, Focused on Business Results and Employee Development

The first step in this phase is to launch it. It is important during initiation to emphasize to everyone concerned that the AAL team experience is not a typical business project; rather, it is a way to meet a business need while also developing workers through on-the-job experience. It can help to remind everyone concerned about the 70-20-10 model in which 70 percent of employee development occurs on the job through work experience, 20 percent occurs through social media and social learning by peer learning, and only 10 percent occurs through planned online, onsite, or blended learning experiences. That well-known 70-20-10 rule comes from the work of Morgan McCall, Robert Eichinger, and Michael Lombardo at the Center for Creative Leadership in the middle of the 1990s (Colman, 2022).

AAL can meet all three of the 70-20-10 model requirements. AAL occurs through practical experiments on the job to solve business problems, meet training challenges, formulate or implement business visions, or achieve business goals. That relates to the 70 percent. It can involve working with peers to get input on the issue confronting the AAL team and experimenting to find solutions. That relates to the 20 percent. It can use planned instruction to enhance AAL team knowledge of matters related to the issue the team members are addressing. That relates to the 10 percent.

Step 2: Plan the Project with Dual Emphasis

In an AAL project team, the team leader usually takes the initiative to create a project plan to guide team actions. However, a project plan alone is not sufficient to meet both the business results requirement and the employee development requirement that typifies AAL. The team facilitator will usually work with the team leader, and the team facilitator will create a plan for employee development during the AAL project. Whereas a team leader or team facilitator could achieve the expectation of focusing on results and on development, it is difficult for one person to achieve that balance on a sustained basis.

When planning for an AAL project, it helps to have two plans: one focused on the project or set results and one focused on achieving employee development goals. Doing that has the advantage of ensuring that an equal balance is placed between work results and employee development.

Step 3: Execute the Project with Dual Emphasis

As an AAL project team executes its project and development plan, the dual emphasis on business results and employee development will be equally emphasized throughout. As the team progresses toward meeting the challenge confronting the team, team discussions will be as much focused on employee development as on business results. One way to do that is to ensure that the team leader and team facilitator are given equal time in team meetings to address the issues on which they separately focus.

Step 4: Monitor and Control the Project with Dual Emphasis

As the AAL team effort is implemented, the Team Leader and Team Facilitator will equally emphasize their respective areas of interest.

Team leaders and team facilitators can do that by creating graphic support tools, such as dashboards or scorecards, to make it easy for AAL team members and team sponsor(s) to see how team progress is being made on work results and on employee development. Team leaders will usually focus on progress on team goals; team facilitators will focus on individual and team learning.

It is possible to devise individual learning plans for the entire AAL team and for individuals on the team (US Office of Personnel Management, 2014). When doing that, team leaders and team facilitators should pay attention to:

■ Development needs pinpointed from team assessments
■ Project goals identified by AAL team sponsor(s)
■ Activities to be carried out to meet needs/goals
■ A timeline for carrying out the activities
■ A budget
■ A responsibility chart to ensure people are clear on what to do during the project.

It helps to do regular pulse checks with the team. Team leaders can do that by simply asking the team sponsor(s) and the team members how they feel the team is progressing in achieving results. Team facilitators can do that by asking about team interaction.

Step 5: Close the Accelerated Action Learning Team Set with Dual Emphasis

When the AAL team reaches its limits in time, money, or effort, equal attention will be devoted to debriefs of how much the team efforts contributed to business results and to team/individual development.

What Role Does Microlearning Play in This Phase?

Several microlearning strategies can be used during an AAL team project to ensure that equal emphasis is placed on achieving business results and developing the AAL team collectively and individually.

One good strategy is for the team leader and team facilitator to discuss this issue in the first meeting of the team. During such a meeting, the team leader can emphasize that his/her role is to focus on achieving the business results, while the team facilitator can emphasize that his/her role is to focus on ensuring that the team is developed collectively and individually. Although it is possible to organize AAL teams without two leaders—that is, the team leader and the team facilitator—the risk in doing it is that something might be lost in the shuffle. There is a temptation to focus only on getting results while ignoring or diminishing the importance of employee development. Doing that defeats the purpose of an AAL team.

There is little difference between a traditional business committee, council, work group, or team and an AAL team that does not emphasize both results and development. The key to AAL is to ensure that equal emphasis is placed on results and development.

A second good strategy is to develop microlearning resources that will encourage learners to make the most of what they learn during the AAL experience. The team facilitator may make resources available to team members to give individuals—and all team members—ideas about how to use their AAL experience to contribute to achieving their career goals (like working toward promotion) or developing their skills in line with upskilling. Works like the classic *Eighty-eight Assignments for Development in Place* (Lombardo and Eichinger, 1989) can give individuals ideas about how they may leverage what they learn from AAL in the future.

A third strategy is for AAL team facilitators to work with the Talent Development function in the organization to come up with ways that individuals and a team can derive the most value from the on-the-job work experiences in which they participate. That is a topic never treated in schools or in formal education. But on-the-job learning strategies are increasingly important for workers as organizations struggle with the need to upskill workers to deal with future organizational challenges and to deal with real-time efforts to keep workers' skills current to meet present organizational and job challenges (Rothwell, 1996).

What Are the Roles of Team Leaders and Team Facilitators in This Phase?

Through various phases team leaders focus on getting work results while team facilitators focus on ensuring that team members learn from their experiences and from each other.

Those roles are emphasized in this phase of the AAL model. If team leaders do their jobs on their teams, the teams are more likely to avoid wasting time and to maximize the results that the team needs. Moves from one experiment to others will be efficient and effective. If team facilitators do their jobs on their teams, the teams are more likely to meet such development objectives as learning from their experiences and learning from each other.

Some organizations will have only one leader on each AAL team. Although that can save time, it may lead to a diminution of achieving results or encouraging collective and team development. Teams will do a good job at getting work results. (That might be called the "default setting" of work on teams.) But the risk is that employee development will be forgotten as team leaders struggle to come in under budget and on time with the results. That will not be AAL; rather, that will be a traditional work team going about business as usual.

How is Reflection Used in This Phase?

Reflection stimulates innovation beyond the business results that the AAL team may secure from experiments; reflection stimulates innovation for team members collectively and individually in how they develop from the AAL experience.

96 ■ *Accelerated Action Learning*

As is true in most phases of AAL, each step of this phase can be a focus for reflection. During the first step of this phase, the team leader and team facilitator can set measurable goals for the project. Setting those goals can stimulate reflection on what is achieved and why. In the second step of this phase, the team facilitator can review any project plans formulated by the team leader and/or team and raise questions about what development plans should be formulated for each project step. In the third step of this phase, the team facilitator can draw attention to employee development issues at every team meeting to discuss AAL team project progress. Doing that should prompt reflection on this important issue rather than leaving it as an afterthought. In the fourth step of this phase, the team facilitator can engage team members to find ways to draw attention to team development. Whereas team leaders may construct dashboards to show the progress of the team toward its AAL goals, team facilitators should prompt reflection during experiments on what the team members learned collectively and individually. In the fifth and final step of this phase, the team facilitator should ensure that collective and individual development is not forgotten as it presents the results of the AAL experience. By doing that, the team facilitator prompts reflection on the past ("What did we learn from our experiments?") and on the future ("What do we need to learn in the future?").

What Should Be Considered for Virtual and Hybrid Settings in This Phase?

The differences between virtual and hybrid settings in AAL should not be much different in this phase. Placing equal emphasis on getting business results and on developing workers on the AAL team should be achievable whether the AAL team meets virtually or in some hybrid format.

But Gera (2013) found significant differences between face-to-face and online groups:

> Virtual teams provide a structure that makes it possible for individuals to work for an organization across time and space. Researchers have found that members of face to face teams are more satisfied, supportive and provide innovative solutions due to self actualizing and constructive style. Members of the virtual teams on the other hand are more prone to conflicts, less satisfied and have inferior

decision making due to passive and aggressive style. There are no significant differences found on the basis of performance.

(p. 13)

Gera does not address mixed groups where some workers are positioned at a central location and others work from home or online.

More recent research has shown that workers perceive they are more productive when working from home. Consider (Stropoli, 2021):

> nearly six out of 10 workers reported being more productive working from home than they expected to be, compared with 14 percent who said they got less done. On average, respondents' productivity at home was 7 percent higher than they expected. Forty percent of workers reported they were more productive at home during the pandemic than they had been when in the office, and only 15 percent said the opposite was true.

How Can This Phase Be Evaluated?

Ultimately, this phase is evaluated based on (1) achievement of business results; and (2) development of AAL team members collectively and individually. The arbiter of the first issue, business results, will be the AAL team sponsor and the team members. The team sponsor will grade the AAL team's performance by whether the team solves the business problem set for it, meets the training challenge it is to achieve, formulates or implements the business vision given to it, or achieves the business goals established for the team. Although the team sponsor, who is usually the one whose budget will pay for the AAL team effort, has an important vote, so too do team members. Do the AAL team members believe they met the measurable goals for the team? Does the team agree with the team sponsor?

The second issue to be evaluated is much more of a question for the AAL team. Do the team members collectively believe they learned something from the experience on the AAL team? Do the team members individually believe they benefited from participation on the team, and in what ways? Answering these questions will help to address how this phase is evaluated.

Avoiding the Most Common Mistakes

What is the most common mistake made in this phase? The answer is simple. The most common mistake is to elevate the importance of the task to be accomplished (solving a problem, meeting a training challenge, formulating/implementing a vision, or achieving a business goal) while minimizing (or altogether forgetting) the development of the AAL team. To avoid this common mistake, it is important to emphasize the equal emphasis placed on getting results and developing workers from the outset. That is an important justification for having two team leaders: one focused on getting results (the team leader) and one focused on development (the team facilitator).

References

Bakker, R. (2010). Taking stock of temporary organizational forms: A systematic review and research agenda. *International Journal of Management Reviews*, *12*, 466–486.

Boskamp, E. (2023). *35+ compelling workplace collaboration statistics: The importance of teamwork*. The Career Experts. https://www.zippia.com/advice/workplace-collaboration-statistics/

Colman, H. (2022, March 1). *70:20:10 learning model: How to enhance it with technology*. ISpring blog. https://www.ispringsolutions.com/blog/70-20-10-learning-model#:~:text=What%20Is%20the%2070%3A20,executives%20about%20their%20learning%20philosophy

Cross, R., Benson, M., Kostal, J., & Milnor, R. (2021, September 27). Collaboration overload is sinking productivity. *Harvard Business Review*. https://hbr.org/2021/09/collaboration-overload-is-sinking-productivity

"Flash" organizations and temporary teams – On the rise? (2017, December 20). https://www.hensonconsultinginternational.com/flash-organizations-and-temporary-teams-on-the-rise/

Gera, S. (2013). Virtual teams versus face to face teams: A review of literature. *IOSR Journal of Business and Management, 11*(2), 1–4.

Lombardo, M., & Eichinger, R. (1989). *Eighty-eight assignments for development in place*. Center for Creative Leadership.

Rothwell, W. (1996). *The self-directed on-the-job learning workshop*. Human Resource Development Press.

Stropoli, R. (2021). *Are we really more productive working from home?* Chicago Booth Review. https://www.chicagobooth.edu/review/are-we-really-more-productive-working-home

U.S. Office of Personnel Management. (2014). *Individual development planning: A guidebook for employees and managers*. The Superintendent of Public Documents.

Exhibit 7.2 A Tool for Placing Equal Emphasis on Business Results and Employee Development

Directions: Use this Worksheet/Tool to guide your thinking when planning an accelerated action learning (AAL) team experience. For each step in this phase of AAL appearing in the left-hand column below, indicate in the right-hand column how your team will ensure that equal emphasis during the AAL project will be placed on achieving business results and on developing workers on the team collectively and individually. There are no absolute "right" or "wrong" answers, though some answers may be better than others—depending on the nature of your organization.

Steps in this Phase of the AAL Project		How Your Team Will Ensure Placing Equal Emphasis on Achieving Business Results and Developing Workers Collectively and Individually during the AAL Project
1	Initiate the project focused on business results and employee development	
2	Plan the project with dual emphasis	
3	Execute the project with dual emphasis	
4	Monitor and control the project with dual emphasis	
5	Close the accelerated action learning team set with dual emphasis	

Chapter 8

Phase 7: Completing the Accelerated Action Learning Set

What is the seventh phase of the accelerated action learning model (AALM)? The seventh phase is the point when AAL team members complete the AAL team project (see Exhibit 8.1). In this phase, team members reach a limitation: they solve the business problem after one or more experiments; they meet a training challenge by analyzing training needs, designing and developing the training, delivering the training, and evaluating results; they formulate and/or implement a business vision; or they achieve a business goal set for the team. The team may fail or simply may run out of time, money, or willingness to continue experimentation.

This chapter opens with a case story that dramatizes the situation when a team has reached the conclusion of the accelerated action learning set. The chapter also examines how the conclusion of an AAL team can be handled, the role that microlearning can play in this phase, and reviews the roles that team leaders and team facilitators can play in this seventh phase. The chapter also examines how individual reflection plays a part in this phase, delineates how virtual and hybrid settings should be considered in this phase, lists common mistakes made in this phase, and offers tips on how to solve, or avoid, those common mistakes. The chapter ends with a tool to facilitate concluding an accelerated action learning set.

 DOI: 10.4324/9781003348658-8

The Accelerated Action Learning Model (AALM)

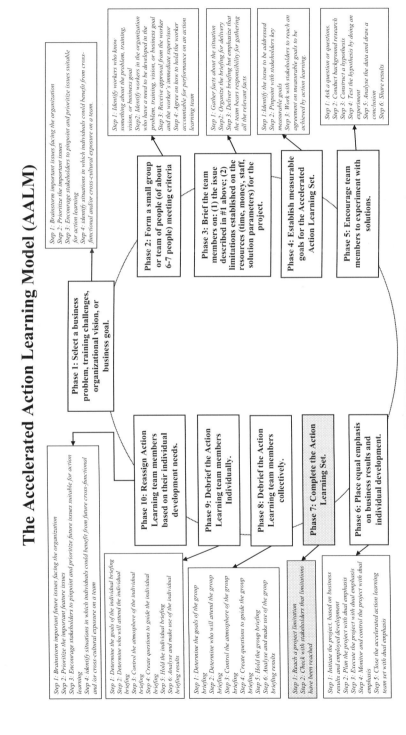

Exhibit 8.1 The Accelerated Action Learning Model (AALM)

Opening Case Story

Martin Higgins is the team leader of an AAL team; Marissa Tumberline is the team facilitator. The team, consisting of five other people who call themselves "the A team," has been working part-time for over a year to discover a way to identify and come up with ways to apply the employment brand of the XYZ corporation. XYZ consists of a chain of retail convenience stores scattered throughout the US East Coast, from Florida in the south to New York State in the north. XYZ has about 300 stores in the coastal states.

XYZ has been having trouble recruiting people. That should not surprise many employers after the global COVID-19 pandemic. The reason: there are roughly 1.5 job openings for every one worker. All employers have been scrambling to find anyone to fill positions.

XYZ is prone to this problem. The company hires recent high school graduates for low-paid jobs in what amounts to a chain of convenience stores with gas stations attached. The work is simple, and the pay is low. Workers are not eager to seek these jobs.

Although company managers hold the philosophy that "a company gets the quality of talent it is willing to pay for," they are resigned to having trouble in recruiting, selecting, onboarding, and retaining good talent. But John Edwards, the Vice President for Human Resources of XYZ, believes the company can do better than the other senior executives believe. He thinks that workers are attracted to XYZ for specific reasons that can be identified. He further believes that workers stay at XYZ for reasons distinct from why they might leave. Having heard of employment branding, by which employers identify why workers are attracted to and remain with their employers, Edwards commissioned an accelerated action learning team to work part-time (two hours per week) to isolate the company's employment brand and to leverage it to its advantage in company efforts to recruit and retain workers.

The team used several experiments in their efforts to find and use employment branding for XYZ. They ran focus groups; they benchmarked the efforts of other convenience store chains to isolate their employment brands; and they ran focus groups of selected company employees. Whereas the team succeeded in what they thought was identifying the company's employment brand—which turned out to be the convenient locations that the company occupied compared with other employers—Edwards was not happy with the results. Edwards, as team sponsor, had an opinion critical in determining whether the team's efforts were acceptable or unacceptable.

When the team members learned that Edwards was not happy with the team's findings, the team members signaled their desire to disband the team and cease any further work. That was the end of this phase of the AAL project.

What Are the Steps in Completing an Action Learning Set?

There are two steps in this phase. First, a team reaches its limitation(s). Second, the members of an AAL team check with the team stakeholders that limitations have been reached. Experimentation ceases and the team begins the eighth phase.

Step 1: Reach a Project Limitation

A limitation is just what it sounds like: it is a limit on the efforts of an AAL team. It means that the AAL team has reached a constraint of time or money. One possible limitation is that the team may actually solve the problem the team was asked to solve; one possible limitation is that the team members give up, noting that the team sees no additional avenues to investigate to solve a problem, prepare training, formulate/implement a vision, or realize a business goal.

Early on in the establishment of an AAL team, the team sponsor and team members should agree on the project limitations that will lead to the cessation of team efforts. Limitations are boundaries. They center around reaching limits on time, money, team willingness to continue experimentation, and even a continuing sponsor (because the loss of a team sponsor to resignation may prompt an AAL set shutdown).

At the outset of the AAL team experience, the AAL team is typically given limits on the time, money, external help, and other resources needed to carry out the project. When the time, money, and help runs out, a limitation is reached and project experimentation ceases.

Step 2: Check with Stakeholders That Limitations Have Been Reached

AAL team members are working for an employer and are under the guidance of a team sponsor. While they can agree that the team has reached its limitation(s), the team may not cease their efforts until the team sponsor and other relevant stakeholders agree with the team assessment. That is why it is necessary for the stakeholders to be consulted before the team is formally decommissioned.

There could be situations in which the AAL team wants to shut down but that team owner(s) or stakeholder(s) do not want the shutdown to occur. In those cases, it is usually worthwhile to hold a meeting to discuss the points of disagreement—and try to determine a way forward.

What Role Does Microlearning Play in This Phase?

Shutting down an AAL team requires more than simply "pulling the plug."

First, a shutdown requires recognition by more people than the AAL team members. The team leader must agree that the project has reached its limits; the team facilitator must agree that the project has reached its limits; the team sponsor must agree that the project has reached its limits; and other stakeholders, who interests are served by the AAL project, must also agree that the project team has reached its limits.

Microlearning can help team members learn how to:

■ Shut down a project
■ Poll stakeholders about their opinions at the end of a project
■ Identify opportunities that may exist beyond the AAL team project for possible efforts by future AAL teams to solve the problem, meet the training challenge, formulate or implement a vision, or achieve business goals
■ Demonstrate the role that real-time, bite-sized learning efforts can play in enhancing real-time innovation and improving solutions to business problems.

Often, a simple web search will yield valuable information for an AAL team to use during an experiment. That should not be forgotten by team leaders or by team facilitators.

What Are the Roles of Team Leaders and Team Facilitators in This Phase?

Team leaders focus on project plans, exerting efforts to bring in the team results on time and under budget. Team facilitators work to ensure that the voices of all team members are heard during the team project and that team members benefit from the employee development opportunities presented to them.

If the team leader and team facilitator agree with team members that the AAL project set limitations have been reached, then the team knows that it is time to dissolve team efforts. The team leader normally initiates contact with the team sponsor and other important stakeholders to consult with them to see if they agree that a team has reached its limits. Shutting down an AAL experience is not just a decision to be made by the team leader, team facilitator, and team members; rather, the team sponsor(s) and team stakeholders must agree.

If there is disagreement between the team members, team sponsor(s), and team stakeholder(s), the team leader and team facilitator must work together to resolve the conflict by finding ways to move forward. It can be a difficult political situation but it is a problem that can be solved.

How Is Reflection Used in This Phase?

Reflection is important at the conclusion of an AAL set. Without reflection, the team members will not benefit by new thinking about what to experiment on or what conclusions should be drawn from the experiments that the AAL team has undertaken.

Key questions can be posed at or near the end of an AAL set:

- What are the signs that the AAL set is reaching its limitations?
- How much time is left until the deadlines? Is it likely that deadlines can be extended?
- How much money is left in the AAL team budget? Can additional funds be secured?
- How much has the AAL team learned collectively so far?
- How much has each AAL team member contributed and learned during the AAL project?
- What possibilities exist for future experiments? (If none can be identified, that is a sign that the AAL project should be shut down.)
- How do AAL team members feel about the AAL project? Is there evidence of burnout?

These and other questions can be posed in regular AAL meetings by the team leader and/or by the team facilitator.

What Should Be Considered for Virtual and Hybrid Settings in This Phase?

When the team reaches its limitations and begins the shutdown, there is often little difference between onsite, online, and hybrid venues for the AAL team. Although more work will be done remotely in the US and probably in many other countries, team leaders and team facilitators must master the ability to manage and facilitate onsite, online, and hybrid teams.

According to *"Statistics"* (2022):

> A survey conducted by Upwork of 1,500 hiring managers found that, due to COVID-19, 61.9% of the companies were planning more remote work now and in the following years to come. Accelerating the remote work trend that has been going on for the past few years. This same report predicts 36.2 million workers or 22% of Americans will be working remotely by the year 2025. This is an 87% increase from pre-pandemic levels. Global Workplace Analytics estimates that 56% of W2 workers or 75 million employers could work from home if their employers allowed it. Global Workplace Analytics estimates that 25–30% of the workforce will work from home for several days a week by the end of 2021.

Thus, those using AAL should be prepared to deal with more online and hybrid workers. Team facilitators must master the skills of virtual group coaching (Rothwell & Park, 2021).

How Can This Phase Be Evaluated?

Evaluation for reaching limitations rests primarily with the team sponsor(s) and team stakeholder(s). The real questions are these:

- Were the limitations on the AAL team, established in early phases, reached?
- Is there insufficient money to continue?
- Is there insufficient time to continue?
- Is there insufficient staff to continue?

- Do team members want to disband/shut down the AAL team?
- Has the business problem been solved if that was the reason for forming the AAL team?
- Has the training challenge, if that was the reason for forming the AAL team, been met?
- Has the business vision, if that was the reason for forming the AAL team, been formulated and implemented?
- Has the business goal been achieved?
- Are team members in agreement that the AAL team should be disbanded?
- Is the team leader in agreement that the AAL team should be disbanded?
- Is the team facilitator in agreement that the AAL team should be disbanded?

If many of the above questions can be answered with a "yes," then the team has reached its limitation(s).

Avoiding the Most Common Mistakes

There are many common mistakes made in this phase.

First, the AAL team members may want to disband the AAL team if the team members feel that the AAL project is interfering too much with their full-time job responsibilities and that the rewards for achieving success on the AAL team project are inadequate to warrant more time and effort. Many AAL team members are keenly aware of what key performance indicators (KPIs) they must meet on their jobs. If the AAL team is not adequately weighted as part of their job responsibilities, then team members will focus on what they are held accountable for doing and will want to remove anything that interferes with meeting their performance targets.

Second, the AAL team members may want to disband prematurely because they think they solved a business problem, met a training challenge, formulated or implemented a vision, or achieved a business goal. But if the team sponsor(s) or important team stakeholders do not agree, then there will be a problem. That problem can be resolved if the team sponsor(s)/stakeholder(s) clarify how they judge the quality of the AAL team's work.

References

Rothwell, W., & Park, C. (2021). *Virtual coaching to improve group relationships: Process consultation reimagined.* Routledge.
Statistics on remote workers that will surprise you. (2022, December 2). https://www.apollotechnical.com/statistics-on-remote-workers/

Exhibit 8.2 A Tool for Deciding on the Shutdown of an Accelerated Action Learning Set

Directions: For each question appearing in the left-hand column below, check a box in the middle column to indicate "Yes," "No," or "Maybe." Then, in the right-hand column, write a brief justification for your accelerated action learning team's viewpoints on how the question in the left-hand column was answered.				
Questions	**Answers**			**The Accelerated Action Learning Team's Justifications for the Answers**
	Yes	**No**	**Maybe**	
1 Were the limitations on the AAL team, established in early phases, reached?				
2 Is there insufficient money to continue?				
3 Is there insufficient time to continue?				
4 Is there insufficient staff to continue?				
5 Do team members want to disband/shut down the accelerated action learning team?				
6 Has the business problem been solved if the problem was the reason for the team to be formed?				

7	Has the training challenge been met if that was the reason for the team to be formed?				
8	Has the business vision been formulated or implemented if that was the reason for the team to be formed?				
9	Has the business goal been achieved?				
10	Are the team members in agreement that the accelerated action learning team should be disbanded?				
11	Is the team leader in agreement that the accelerated action learning team should be disbanded?				
12	Is the team facilitator in agreement that the accelerated action learning team should be disbanded?				
13	Are there other questions to be considered before the team is shut down or disbanded?				

Chapter 9

Phase 8: Debriefing the Accelerated Action Learning Team Members Collectively

The eighth phase is the point when AAL team members collectively debrief the AAL team project (see Exhibit 9.1). In this phase, team members meet to discuss what the AAL team accomplished, what is yet to be accomplished (perhaps by future AAL teams), and what the members of the AAL learned during the AAL team experience.

This chapter opens with a case story that dramatizes the situation when a team is brought together for a debriefing. The chapter also examines how the debriefing of an AAL team can be handled, the role that microlearning can play in this phase, and reviews the roles that team leaders and team facilitators can play in this eighth phase. The chapter also examines how individual reflection plays a part in this phase, delineates how virtual and hybrid settings should be considered in this phase, lists common mistakes made in this phase, and offers tips on how to solve, or avoid, those common mistakes. The chapter ends with a tool to facilitate an AAL team debriefing.

Opening Case Story

John Lormax is CEO of the Lormax corporation, which he founded in 1972. Lormax is now 78 years old. He founded an AAL team to explore ways to increase the sales of the company's watches. Watch sales for Lormax have

DOI: 10.4324/9781003348658-9

The Accelerated Action Learning Model (AALM)

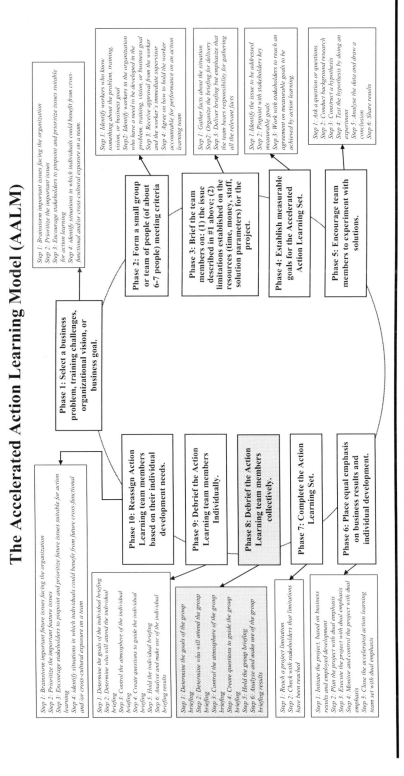

Exhibit 9.1   The Accelerated Action Learning Model (AALM)

suffered over the years due to increased competition, imports, and a decline in customers who want to wear a wristwatch.

Lormax's AAL team consisted of five people, one of whom (Martin Normal) served as team leader, and one of whom (Harold Gunderson) served as team facilitator. The team members represented different functional areas of the plan and different layers on the organization chart. The team was assigned full-time to increase sales, and the team carried out five experiments. The team was largely successful because sales of watches increased 18 percent due to the enhancements that the AAL team experimented with.

Lormax was thus the team sponsor for the AAL team, which called itself the "Time Team."

As the team met its challenge (in the important opinions of the team and Lormax), the team was disbanded. But, at the last meeting, the AAL team went through a collective debriefing.

The team facilitator was aware that a one-hour debriefing was limited in time. The team facilitator focused on a few simple questions:

■ What does the team feel were the major results achieved by the team?
■ What does the team feel that the team collectively learned from the AAL experience? (Do not discuss your individual learning; rather, focus on the collective learnings of the team.)
■ If the team continued, what would be the focus of future experiments and why?

The debriefing was held, and the team sponsor attended. Team members were enthusiastic in congratulating themselves on what they had achieved. They noted that future experiments should focus on how to compete against the increasing flow of imports and how to compete against so many distinctive watches available through Amazon and other online merchants.

What Are the Steps for Debriefing an Action Learning Team Collectively?

Step 1: Determine the Goals of the Group Briefing

As a good training program has measurable training objectives to ensure that learners leave planned instruction with targets met, a good briefing has measurable goals to be achieved. Those goals should be related to examining the business results achieved by the AAL project team during the action learning set and evaluating how well the AAL team members collectively achieved their individual development goals.

To address these goals, complete these sentences:

■ Upon completing the briefing, the AAL team will have described what measurable business goals were achieved from the AAL team experience ...

■ Upon completing the briefing, the AAL team will have described what measurable employee development goals for the team collectively were achieved ...

Step 2: Determine Who Will Attend the Group Briefing

An AAL team debriefing will typically include the team leader, the team facilitator, and all team members. Additionally, an AAL team meeting will also include the team sponsor.

Other stakeholders may be included. They should be identified and contacted well before the scheduled briefing. A briefing agenda should be prepared and distributed in advance to ensure that the briefing time is effectively used. The agenda should place equal emphasis on the business results achieved during the AAL project and the employee development that occurred.

Step 3: Control the Atmosphere of the Group Briefing

The atmosphere, otherwise known as the climate, of the group briefing refers to the "psychological feeling" of the briefing. Is it confrontational? Is it factually focused? Is it emotionally laden?

Usually, the best atmosphere will be factually focused. Team members should focus on the business results achieved and on the employee development goals achieved. Value-laden or emotional language should generally be avoided.

Step 4: Create Questions to Guide the Group Briefing

Questions can help to guide the AAL team by providing general guidance. However, efforts should avoid so-called leading questions that assume some condition. A classic example of a leading question is the well-known example "When did you stop telling lies?" It assumes a condition exists that may defy reality.

It is better to pose open-ended questions to AAL team members that will stimulate their thinking and encourage other participants in the briefing to think about what results the team achieved and how well team members learned and developed from their experience.

Examples of typical questions to pose during an AAL team debrief might include:

- Who was involved in the AAL team experiments, and what results were achieved from the accelerated action learning team set?
- What results were achieved?
- When (over what time frame) were results achieved?
- Where (in what locations) were results achieved?
- Why was the AAL project undertaken, and what business results stemmed from it?
- How did the AAL team approach the project, and what did team members learn from the experience collectively?

Of course, some team facilitators might prefer to use a questionnaire to gather data from the AAL team to evaluate the AAL experience. The questionnaire can be distributed to the AAL team before the debriefing, the results compiled, and then fed back to the AAL team to stimulate thoughts about the experience. It is an approach to organization development (Jones & Rothwell, 2017).

Exhibit 9.2 Action Learning—Evaluation

Name:

Organization:

PRE-START

What kind of issues are you facing at work that you hope accelerated action learning will help you to resolve?

1.

2.

3.

How would you rate your own accelerated action learning-related skills at the start of this program?

Skill	Rating				
Listening behind a person's words for underlying beliefs, values, or concerns					
Posing questions that enable a person to think more deeply or broadly					
Creating solutions for complex issues that lack a single right answer					
Taking action confidently in situations that feel unclear, fluid, or ambiguous					
Awareness of my own assumptions and the potential impacts of my behaviour					

1. Aware ("I know that this is important")
2. Basic ("I can do this with support")
3. Competent ("I can do this well in my own job")
4. Distinguished ("Others look to me for support in this area")
5. Expert ("I provide expertise in this area externally")

POST-SET

How would you rate your own accelerated action learning-related skills at the end of this program?

Skill	Rating				
Listening behind a person's words for underlying beliefs, values, or concerns					
Posing questions that enable a person to think more deeply or broadly					
Creating solutions for complex issues that lack a single right answer					

Taking action confidently in situations that feel unclear, fluid, or ambiguous					
Awareness of my own assumptions and the potential impacts of my behaviour					

    1. Aware ("I know that this is important")
    2. Basic ("I can do this with support")
    3. Competent ("I can do this well in my own job")
    4. Distinguished ("Others look to me for support in this area")
    5. Expert ("I provide expertise in this area externally")

Overall, what have you found most useful about this accelerated action learning set experience?

In what ways have you handled issues at work differently since taking part in this set?

To what degree would you attribute your development to what you have learned through this program (fully/partially/not at all)?

On a scale of 1 to 10 (1 = low, 10 = high), how far has this accelerated action learning set experience met your hopes and expectations?

What would make the biggest improvement to similar accelerated action learning programs in future?

Source: Nick Wright, Director, Action Learning Associates, UK www.actionl earningassociates.co.uk. *Used with permission.*

Step 5: Hold the Group Briefing

In this step, the debriefing for the AAL team is carried out.
When a group is brought together, unexpected events can occur despite the best planning efforts. Although it is highly desirable to have an agenda to guide a group debriefing, groups may be subject to:

■ One or more members going off on a tangent
■ One or more members dominating the discussion
■ People becoming emotional
■ People lying about what the group achieved.

There are many ways the group debriefing can go wrong. However, an effective debriefing is well planned. The team leader and team facilitator have planned for a well-organized event (*"Guide to event debrief,"* n.d.).

It is a good idea to have meeting minutes of an AAL team debrief to ensure that important ideas are captured for future reference (Bárcenas, 2023).

Step 6: Analyze and Make Use of the Group Briefing Results

After the AAL team debriefing is finished, the minutes should be retained. If a similar problem occurs and a new AAL team is constituted to address that problem, it is useful to analyze the minutes from previous AAL teams and make use of the group briefing results.

What Role Does Microlearning Play in This Phase?

Microlearning may have a limited role in this phase of AAL.
Team members can prepare for the briefing event by using microlearning to make the meeting most effective. Meetings are notorious for being badly managed and poorly handled. Consider (Flynn, 2023):

■ Every week, around 55 million meetings are held in the United States. That equates to at least 11 million per day and over one billion per year.

- The average worker spends at least three hours per week in meetings, with 30 percent indicating that they spend more than five hours per week in meetings.
- Meetings take up around 15 percent of an organization's time, *with polls revealing that 71 percent of those sessions are ineffective.*
- Unproductive meetings cost an estimated $37 billion per year.
- Unproductive meetings take up an average of 31 hours per month for employees.
- In-person meetings are preferred by 47 percent of employees. This is significant, given that 90 percent of Americans desire fewer meetings in the workplace.
- Over 55 percent of remote workers believe that the bulk of meetings "could have been done via email."
- This is the most popular pet peeve among employees. Other annoyances include "people with loud background noises," as well as unprepared individuals and off-topic conversations.
- During online meetings, 15 percent of remote workers do housework.
- People also engage in a variety of other distracting activities, such as babysitting, pet care, going for a jog, and so on. Although this is not most cases, they account for a little under 10 percent of responders.
- Zoom's unique global visitors fell from 1.8 million in January 2022 to 1.3 million in May 2022.

Briefings can be improved if team members know how to participate more effectively and how to contribute to greatest effect.

Microlearning in this phase can be used to best effect if team members have been briefed on how to make meetings and briefings most effective and then apply those principles to the AAL team debriefing.

What Are the Roles of Team Leaders and Team Facilitators in This Phase?

To prepare for a briefing, the team leader may need more information in a quick, practical format about how to run briefings and how to focus attention on what results the team, working together, collectively achieved. That information should be summarized in the session.

To prepare for a briefing, the team facilitator may need more information on how to pose questions to stimulate the team's thinking on what the team learned from the AAL experience. When running a meeting, a team facilitator should be prepared to pose questions to the AAL team and keep the discussion on track. When participants stray into tangential topics, team facilitators are well advised to use a "parking lot" (flipchart page posted on the wall to write topics that are off-target for the meeting.)

The team facilitator should take notes during the meeting—or else delegate that chore to a team member—and then remember to circulate those meeting minutes after the briefing. That can help participants in the meeting remember what topics were discussed in the AAL team debriefing.

How Is Reflection Used in This Phase?

Reflection is critical in this phase. For this phase to be effective, AAL team members must be prompted to reflect on such questions as these:

- What did the AAL team accomplish?
- What did the AAL team learn from experience in their experiments?
- What should the AAL team learn if they remain together?
- How well did the AAL team members work together?
- How could the AAL team work together more effectively if they remain together?

Each question above can prompt collective reflection from the team when they meet.

What Should Be Considered for Virtual and Hybrid Settings in This Phase?

There can be a different feeling from team debriefings if held onsite, online, or in a hybrid format.

To ensure that debriefings are run effectively when conducted online, follow the guidelines below (*"Effectively including online participants,"* 2020):

Setup

- Check that the equipment is up to the task, especially that there is good audio and, preferably, video.

- Ensure that a technical expert is present to ensure that everything is working properly onsite and to assist online participants with any issues that may arise.
- Make a practice run first!
- Make it simple for everyone to recognize one other—if you don't already know each other, try providing a list of images and huge nameplates that online participants can read and visibly name identifiers for online participants.
- Determine whether any auxiliary technology (e.g., Google Docs) will be used ahead of time and ensure that everyone has access to it.
- Plan before the briefing and think through small-group tasks.

Tips for onsite configuration

- Ensure that the screen depicting the online participants involves them in the meeting; for example, onsite attendees should not be seated with their backs to the screen.
- Delegate someone to manage what online participants see and to fully use the technology. For example, if online participants can see only part of the meeting room, make sure the camera moves to take in where the discussion is taking place and, if there is a zoom capacity, zoom in on the person speaking.
- Delegate this task to someone who is not a meeting attendee so they may devote their complete attention to it.

Suggestions for online setup

- Make sure your computer's audio is up to the task. If it isn't, get a microphone.
- Use headphones to improve your hearing skills; make sure they are comfy, especially during long meetings.
- Examine your on-screen appearance. Cameras placed into computers frequently display you from an unflattering angle; consider investing in a second camera you can gaze directly into. Adjust the camera distance and angle such that your face is in the center of the screen and of a reasonable size (not too little or too large). Consider what viewers will see behind you.

Advice for Onsite Attendees

- Make room for online players to participate.
- Make eye contact with both online and in-person participants.
- Keep an eye on how the online participants are doing. This can be accomplished through regular check-ins, including monitoring the chat (commenting or messaging) system, as well as a buddy system that pairs online and onsite participants, who communicate during breaks and via chat or e-mail during the meeting.
- Record shared thoughts in a form that everyone can access:
- Use inclusive technology, such as having someone record ideas on their computer, which is projected into the room and screen-shared with online participants.
- Online participants cannot read what is written on a whiteboard or flip chart. If you must use a whiteboard or flip chart, appoint someone to take images and share them with the online participants.
- Organize a procedure for filling in online participants on key onsite conversations outside of the meeting, for example, as during dinner or lunch.

How Can This Phase Be Evaluated?

Evaluation of this phase can occur before, during, after, and long after the AAL debriefing experience.

Before the debriefing, the AAL team members can be surveyed about what they collectively learned from the experience. The survey results can yield valuable information that can then be fed back to the team sponsor, team stakeholders, and team members and discussed at the debriefing. That may lead to a more efficient and effective use of time in the debriefing.

During the debriefing AAL team members may be pointedly asked to evaluate the AAL experience. They may even be asked about accelerated action learning and how much other people and other teams could benefit from similar experiences. That information can prompt corporate culture change to make AAL an important feature of the organization.

Participants at the debriefing may also be given a survey so they need not voice their views publicly. If trust is an issue in the organization, surveys may be a good way to prompt more candid responses.

After the debriefing, the AAL team may be surveyed or interviewed about the collective results and/or learning they believe the entire team collectively experienced.

Long after the AAL team experience, the AAL team members may be polled about the on-the-job impact of the team experience. Did the AAL team project have a long-term impact on the organization?

Avoiding the Most Common Mistakes

The most common mistake made in this phase of AAL is to skip the team debrief. In some organizations, team sponsors and team stakeholders may grade the quality of the effort solely by the business results achieved. They may not pay much attention to the value of the AAL team effort as a process for addressing organizational problems, training challenges, business visions, or organizational goals.

To avoid this common mistake, team leaders and team facilitators should commit to having a collective team debrief at the end of the experience. When their immediate supervisors forget or else discourage a collective debrief, the team leader and team facilitator should mount compelling arguments for the debrief.

References

Bárcenas, M. (2023, April 18). How to write meeting minutes: Best practices (+4 templates). *Fellow.* https://fellow.app/blog/meetings/meeting-minutes-example -and-best-practices/?utm_source=google&utm_medium=cpc&utm_campaign =Dynamic_Campaign_USA_BIZ_WS&utm_term=-&utm_content=649858190068 &adgroupid=123305726821&placement=&gclid=CjwKCAjwpayjBhAnEiwA-7ena -JrAI28FSjvHVINfdxm_y2j1c62lZPhlZl-QNnNE07X_P-YIEozhRoCiCkQAvD _BwE

Effectively including online participants in onsite meetings. (2020, March 24). Integration and Implementation Insights. https://i2insights.org/2020/03/24/ effective-online-plus-onsite-meetings/

Flynn, J. (2023, February 14). *28+ incredible meeting statistics: Virtual, zoom, in-person meetings and productivity.* Zippia. https://www.zippia.com/advice/ meeting-statistics/

Guide to event debrief: How to improve your event and your team's performance. (n.d.). https://superevent.com/blog/guide-event-debrief-improve-event-teams -performance/

Jones, M., & Rothwell, W. (2017). (Eds.). *Evaluating organization development: How to ensure and sustain the successful transformation.* Productivity Press.

Exhibit 9.3 A Tool to Guide a Collective Accelerated Action Learning Team Debriefing

Directions: Use this worksheet/tool to guide the discussion in an accelerated action learning team debriefing. For each question appearing in the left-hand column below, record the answers from the AAL team.	
Questions for the Accelerated Action Learning Team (to be Posed by the Team Facilitator)	**Notes from the Accelerated Action Learning Team Debriefing**
1 What did the accelerated action learning team accomplish?	
2 What did the AAL team learn collectively from experience from the team experiments?	
3 What should the AAL team learn in the future if the team remained together?	
4 How well did the AAL team members work together?	
5 How could the AAL team work together more effectively in the future if they remain together?	

Chapter 10

Phase 9: Debriefing the Accelerated Action Learning Team Members Individually

What is the ninth phase of the accelerated action learning model (AALM)? The ninth phase is the point where AAL team members are individually debriefed. In this phase, the team facilitator meets to discuss what each person learned from the AAL experience and what everyone on the AAL team needs to learn (see Exhibit 10.1).

This chapter opens with a case story that dramatizes the situation when team members are individually debriefed. The chapter also examines how the debriefing of an AAL team can be handled, the role that microlearning can play in this phase, and the roles that team leaders and team facilitators can play in this ninth phase. The chapter also examines how individual reflection plays a part in this phase, delineates how virtual and hybrid settings should be considered in this phase, lists common mistakes made in this phase, and offers tips on how to solve, or avoid, those common mistakes. The chapter ends with a tool to facilitate individual debriefings of individual members of an AAL.

Opening Case Story

John Nicholson is the team facilitator of an accelerated action learning team working for nearly a year on ways to improve how talent was acquired. The

DOI: 10.4324/9781003348658-10

The Accelerated Action Learning Model (AALM)

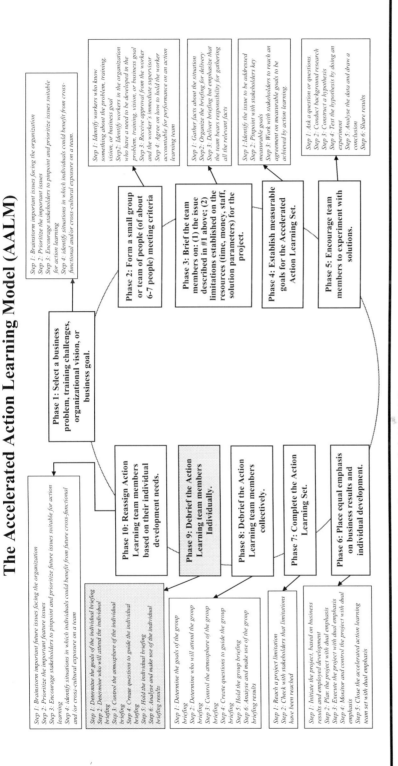

Exhibit 10.1   The Accelerated Action Learning Model (AALM)

five-member team succeeded in increasing the applicant flow to the organization and the percentage of job applicants hired from those who were interviewed. The AAL team experience was a great success.

But the team members were a fractious group. They were always fighting. Although drawn from different levels on the organization chart and from different functional areas of the organization, the team members did not seem able to agree on anything. They even joked that they could not agree on the color of the sky or the color of the ocean. That made the AAL team experience less than satisfactory to the individual team members.

Nicholson faced the task in this phase of debriefing everyone on the team about the AAL experience. He did not look forward to it because he expected to hear about the great success in achieving business results and the great failure in learning how to work together successfully.

Nicholson had to agree with this assessment. His own experience on the team was mixed. Even Nicholson argued with Lori Michaels, the team leader. Lori was always interested in forcing team members to move faster so the team could meet deadlines and was also arguing about spending so that the team could come in under budget. Nicholson was more interested in ensuring that the team members learned from each other and that they were poised at the end of the experience to be clear on what development each team member needed next.

What Are the Steps for Debriefing an Action Learning Team Individually?

For the ninth phase of accelerated action learning to be carried out successfully, the team must be individually debriefed. There are six steps in this phase. They are:

- *Step 1*: Determine the goals of the individual briefing
- *Step 2*: Determine who will attend the individual briefing
- *Step 3*: Control the atmosphere of the individual briefing
- *Step 4*: Create questions to guide the individual briefing
- *Step 5*: Hold the individual briefing
- *Step 6*: Analyze and make use of the individual briefing results.

This section of the chapter will review each step of this phase.

Step 1: Determine the Goals of the Individual Briefings

Why are individual briefings conducted? The answer to that question should be clear—or else higher-level managers may want to slash the use of company time for what they might regard as a frivolous activity.

But a collective group debriefing will often not capture the key points learned from an AAL team experience. Some individuals may not feel comfortable describing their individual conclusions or feelings about the team in a team meeting. That is especially true if their comments bear on the performance or the behavior of other team members.

At minimum, an individual team briefing should explore such issues as:

■ What were the major results or benefits of participating in the AAL project from the individual's standpoint?
■ What future benefits could be realized by future AAL project participation?
■ How did participation in the team experience lead to the development of each team member?
■ What additional development needs did each team member identify because of participation in the AAL project?

Step 2: Determine Who Will Attend the Individual Briefings

Each team member should attend individual briefings. Typically, the team facilitator will lead the individual debriefings with each of the members—including the team leader. Team facilitators should be well-equipped to reflect on their own participation in achieving business results and in identifying future development needs for themselves.

Step 3: Control the Atmosphere of the Individual Briefings

Individual debriefings should be carried out in confidence. Individuals should not be worried that what they say will be fed back to others on the team or to their immediate supervisors in the organization. If a need exists to feedback information to others, that requirement should at least be communicated to the individual with that information.

Great care should be taken in granting unrestricted confidentiality. Should a team member say, "If I tell you something, will you keep it in strict confidence?", if the person conducting the debriefing assents to that request, there could be a problem if a law was broken or if company policy was violated. Sometimes, revealing information may be required by law—as in sexual harassment or other legal violations.

If the team facilitator conducts the individual briefings, s/he will need to establish rapport and maintain a reputation for keeping confidence.

Step 4: Create Questions to Guide the Individual Briefings

Individual briefings, like collective AAL team briefings, should be guided by questions. Since most individual briefings will be conducted over one hour or less, they need to be focused and designed to yield the most important information.

The most important questions to pose in individual briefings include:

- What results do you feel the AAL team secured, and what part did you play?
- What results should future AAL teams work to secure?
- How do you feel you were developed from the AAL team experience?
- Based on your experience on the AAL team, what additional development do you feel you need? Why do you feel that way?
- What other issues do you feel are worth noting?

Step 5: Hold the Individual Briefings

The individual briefings should be conducted as soon as possible after the AAL team ceases its efforts. People forget important information in a short time. Long delays in conducting briefings will mean that individuals forget important information and lose keen insights from their experiences.

Step 6: Analyze and Make Use of the Individual Briefing Results

The team facilitator should analyze and feedback the results of the individual briefings to the AAL team, team sponsor(s), and any stakeholders who depend on or are affected by the AAL teamwork. Only general summaries should be fed back—not the exact words of individuals, which might reveal their identities.

The results of individual briefings can set future targets for future AAL team projects and identify individual development needs of workers who were on the AAL team.

What Role Does Microlearning Play in This Phase?

Team facilitators may find it helpful to consult microlearning events related to conducting briefings. Such material is available. Examples might include infographics on how to conduct meetings/briefings, videos on effective ways to lead meetings or pose important questions, online resources on analyzing interview results and developing themes across interviews, and much more.

In the spirit of microlearning, participants may be asked during debriefings what microlearning experiences might have helped achieve better AAL results or contributed to more effective employee development.

What Are the Roles of Team Leaders and Team Facilitators in This Phase?

Team facilitators play a critical role in this phase. They are often the ones tasked to carry out individual briefings, transcribe interview notes, analyze the themes, and feed them back to team members. Team leaders may set deadlines and identify those who should receive the results from the collective team briefings and the individual team briefings.

There is a possibility that the team could actually hold two separate individual debriefings. One could focus on the AAL team's results; a different one could focus on employee development needs met and/or identified for future action. The team leader would focus on the results; the team facilitator would focus on employee development.

How is Reflection Used in This Phase?

Reflection is critical in realizing benefits from experience and learning. Individuals derive little benefit from their experiences if they do not reflect on them. Individual briefings provide an important venue for encouraging individual reflection. That is one argument for ensuring that such debriefings occur rather than eliminating them to save time. The questions posed by team facilitators during individual debriefings will spark self-reflection and may provide useful insights that can be explored in future AAL team projects.

What Should Be Considered for Virtual and Hybrid Settings in This Phase?

Where and how individual debriefings are conducted can influence what results are obtained. It is not clear whether people are more inclined to speak when they are in virtual settings or in hybrid (some online and some onsite) settings. That may affect how individual debriefings are best conducted.

How Can This Phase Be Evaluated?

Individual debriefings can be evaluated before, during, and after they are conducted.

People will be more open about their insights with those they trust. If team facilitators establish trusting relationships with team members, they are more likely to get useful information during and after the AAL team experience is conducted. Much hinges on how well team members trust the team facilitator.

Avoiding the Most Common Mistakes

The most common mistake made in conducting individual debriefings is yielding to the temptation to save time by not carrying them out. Although that will lead to short-term savings, it will lose the benefits of capturing the insights of the individual participants soon after the experience. Important insights are best captured immediately following events and experiences.

Exhibit 10.2 A Tool to Guide an Individual Accelerated Action Learning Team Debriefing

Directions: The team facilitator may use this tool to guide an individual debriefing at the end of an AAL experience. For each question appearing in the left-hand column below, the team facilitator can write notes from each individual in the right-hand column below.
Name of the Team Facilitator
Date of the Individual Debriefing

Questions for Individuals in an AAL Debriefing	Notes
1	What results do you feel the AAL team secured, and what part did you play?	
2	What results should future AAL teams work to secure in the future?	
3	How do you feel that you were developed from the AAL team experience?	
4	Based on your experience on the AAL team, what additional development do you feel you need? Why do you feel that way?	
5	What other issues do you feel are worth noting?	

Chapter 11

Phase 10: Reassigning Accelerated Action Learning Team Members Based on Their Individual Development Needs

What is the tenth and final phase of the accelerated action learning model (AALM)? The tenth phase is the point where AAL team members can be reassigned to other AAL teams based on the needs of the business and their individual development needs (see Exhibit 11.1). At this point, AAL has come full circle, and team members find themselves on new teams to attack new issues. Learning is continuous.

This chapter opens with a case story that dramatizes the situation when team members are reassigned to new teams. This chapter also examines how reassignments to new AAL teams are handled, the role that microlearning can play in this phase, and reviews the roles that team leaders and team facilitators can play in this tenth phase. The chapter also examines how individual reflection plays a part in this phase, delineates how virtual and hybrid settings should be considered in this phase, lists common mistakes made in this phase, and offers tips on how to solve, or avoid, those common mistakes. The chapter ends with a tool to facilitate individual reassignments based on individual development needs.

    DOI: 10.4324/9781003348658-11

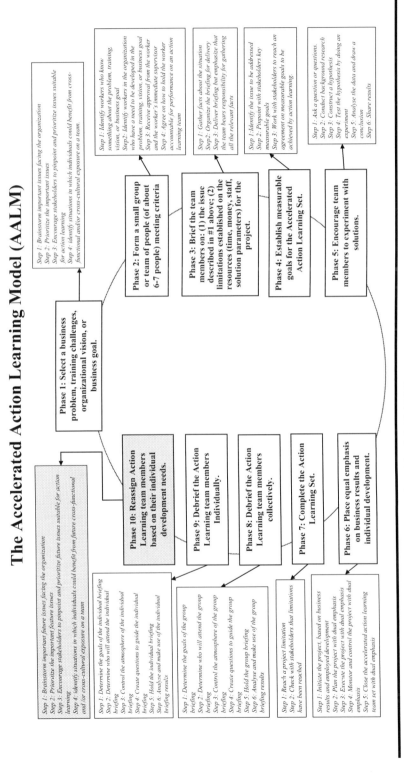

Exhibit 11.1   The Accelerated Action Learning Model (AALM)

Opening Case Story

Pippa Newington is a team facilitator on an AAL team working for the Newcastle corporation.

Newcastle is a long-haul trucking firm with hundreds of large semi-trailer trucks that ship goods around the US.

Newcastle has long had a problem. The truckers working for Newcastle want to remain awake for many hours while on their trips. That violates the US Department of Transportation (DOT) rule:

> The DOT 14-hour rule details how long commercial drivers can work during a 24-hour period. The rule dictates that drivers must fit all of their driving time for the day into a 14-hour shift. They must then take a mandatory 10-hour off-duty period after the 14 consecutive hours on duty.

Various State governments have also issued restrictions on overnight driving for long-haul truckers.

Newcastle's AAL team was tasked with finding ways to encourage truckers to follow the rules and abide by the restrictions. The AAL team was largely successful since a percentage of truckers working for Newcastle did cut back their all-nighters while the AAL team was working and was experimenting with ways to encourage compliance with the rules.

Now that the AAL team has reached its limitations—that is, the experiments succeeded—the team members have been debriefed collectively and individually. It is time to consider reassigning the team members to new AAL teams where they can be further developed in line with the skills each individual team member needs.

What Are the Steps for Reassigning an Accelerated Action Learning Team Collectively?

There are four steps in this phase. Covered in this part, they are:

- *Step 1*: Brainstorm important future issues facing the organization
- *Step 2*: Prioritize the important future issues

- *Step 3*: Encourage stakeholders to pinpoint and prioritize future issues suitable for action learning
- *Step 4*: Identify situations in which individuals could benefit from future cross-functional and/or cross-cultural exposure on a team.

These steps are treated in this section of this chapter.

Step 1: Brainstorm Important Future Issues Facing the Organization

To reassign AAL team members to future AAL teams to meet the development needs of members of the future teams, it is first necessary to identify issues to be addressed by future AAL teams. In this first step of this phase, organizational leaders must periodically identify business problems, training challenges, visions to be formulated or implemented, or business goals to be achieved. They should not be routine or considered merely for employee development; rather, these issues should be genuine issues confronting the business, should warrant attention, and should be suitable for getting business results and developing workers.

Step 2: Prioritize the Important Future Issues

Organizational leaders should identify important, emerging issues. These issues can then be the basis for AAL teams. Working to address those needs can help members of future AAL teams to learn through work experience.

Step 3: Encourage Stakeholders to Pinpoint and Prioritize Future Issues Suitable for Accelerated Action Learning

Stakeholders are those with a stake in the success (or failure) of AAL teams. Stakeholders may include workers, the workers' immediate supervisors, HR professionals, family members of AAL team members, and many other people affected by the results of AAL team action. Stakeholders should be given some say in identifying issues worthy of AAL team action and prioritizing those issues warranting action.

Step 4: Identify Situations in Which Individuals Could Benefit from Future Cross-Functional and/ or Cross-Cultural Exposure on a Team

Not all issues confronting any organization will be suitable for AAL. Some business problems are important and warrant action. But solving those problems may be straightforward but will not develop workers on AAL teams who could be tasked to solve them. AAL must focus on problems that meet the dual standard of being of real import to the organization while also presenting an opportunity for employee development.

What Role Does Microlearning Play in This Phase?

There is almost always a role that microlearning can play when reassigning team members to new teams. If an AAL team member feels that he or she needs further development following an AAL team experience, then microlearning can shed light on the employee development needs and shed light on what that need might be and the issues on that topic that might have a bearing for the team member.

What Are the Roles of Team Leaders and Team Facilitators in This Phase?

Team leaders can point out what AAL team members did on their AAL team. Their focus is on task performance when individuals serve on a team. But team facilitators are the best judges of what additional employee development needs that individuals may have that stemmed from an AAL team experience. The team members themselves must also be consulted on their own development needs.

How is Reflection Used in This Phase?

Reflection strengthens the bonds between learning experiences in AAL sets. Reflective learning allows learners to step back from their learning experience, allowing them to develop critical thinking skills and improve future performance by analyzing what they have learned and how far they have progressed. Reflection is related to casting a look back into the past and evaluating the past to learn from what happened and possibly avoid repeating past mistakes again. However, it is increasingly associated with reflecting on action, which includes analyzing thoughts and feelings, seeking insights, and optimizing self-awareness, which are directly related to identity development.

What Should Be Considered for Virtual and Hybrid Settings in This Phase?

People may interact as they do their work—or participate in AAL sets. They may work virtually; they may work face-to-face; and they may work in hybrid formats in which people are in a central office while others work from home (or from other locales, such as coffee shops or even their automobiles).

Reassignments to future AAL teams do not differ from other work experiences. If people want to work from home, they can interact with their AAL teammates by virtual means.

How Can This Phase Be Evaluated?

It is imperative when evaluating this phase to ensure that people assigned to AAL teams stand to benefit from what they can learn. For instance, if a company needs a new budget system, workers with backgrounds in accounting might be assigned to work on devising a new budget system. But that does not necessarily mean that team members will be exposed to valuable new experiences. AAL requires participants on AAL teams to possess skills that can help solve problems but must also require that the participants stand to learn something of value from the experience.

Avoiding the Most Common Mistakes

The most common mistake made in this phase is to assign people to teams for the wrong reasons. For instance, if a supervisor has a worker that the supervisor does not like, the supervisor may be tempted to assign the worker to an AAL team to remove the worker from the workplace. That is not a good reason to move an employee to an AAL team. Team leaders, team facilitators, and even team sponsors should watch for occasions like that and appeal to higher authority to overturn the placement of the wrong people to AAL teams.

Exhibit 11.2 A Tool to Guide Reassigning Accelerated Action Learning Team Members

Directions: Use this worksheet to guide decision-making about how to reassign accelerated action learning team members. For each question appearing in the left-hand column below, write your answers in the right-hand column. There are no "right" or "wrong" answers in any absolute sense. But there may be some answers that are better than others.

Names of the workers who served on Accelerated Action Learning Teams

Today's Date	
Questions	**Answers**
1	What problems, training challenges, visions, or goals to achieve confront the organization?	
2	Who participated in the immediate past on an accelerated action learning team?	
3	Which team members would benefit most from each issue identified in answer to Question 1 above?	
4	What learning should each team member, listed under number 3 above, seek and why should he/she seek that learning?	
5	Are there other questions that should be considered? If so, what are they, and why are they important?	

Chapter 12

Reflections on Accelerated Action Learning (AAL)

This chapter opens with a case story that summarizes all the phases in accelerated action learning (AAL). This chapter also explains how AAL can be made to move faster, summarizes the advantages and disadvantages of AAL, describes how AAL teams may be made into self-organizing teams, reviews the important relationship between AAL and talent deployment, reviews the barriers to AAL and how to overcome them, examines the analytical and creative approaches to experimentation in accelerated action learning, reviews the common mistakes or problems in AAL teams, discusses how action learning teams can carry out experimentation, and reviews Kolb's learning cycle and AAL.

Summary Case Story: Accelerated Action Learning (AAL) in Manufacturer A G Poindexter

This case study illustrates how AAL is used.

Summary of the Steps in AAL

Consider that the steps in traditional action learning are: (1) select a business problem, training challenge, organizational vision, or business goal; (2) form a small group or team of people (of about six to seven people); (3) brief the team members on the issues and limitations established by the resources

DOI: 10.4324/9781003348658-12

for the project; (4) establish measurable goals for the action learning set; (5) encourage team members to experiment with solutions; (6) place equal emphasis on business results and individual development; (7) complete the action learning set; (8) debrief the action learning team members collectively; (9) debrief the action learning team members individually; and (10) reassign action learning team members based on their individual development needs.

Introduction to the Case Story Example

The A G Poindexter Company, a manufacturing company, had been facing a significant problem of high employee turnover rates. The company's senior leaders tried several strategies to tackle the problem, but none worked effectively. **CEO Gordon Smithson** implemented an action learning program to address this issue.

Forming the Team for the Action Learning Set

The company formed a small team of six individuals from different departments to work on this project: **Larry Michelson** was the Vice President of Manufacturing; **Maria Tylor**, the company's Director of Compensation; **Wu Chang**, a supervisor in the marketing division; **Ferris Buehler**, a manager in the Finance Division of the company; **Vera Wang**, a customer service representative; and **Abigail Morton**, a secretary in the executive offices. Tylor was appointed team facilitator, and Buehler was appointed team leader.

Briefing the Team

Smithson himself briefed the team on the turnover problem and the resources for the project. He described the company's efforts so far to address turnover, expressing disappointment that no efforts so far had proven effective.

Establishing Measurable Goals

The team was also given measurable goals—reduce employee turnover rate to 20 percent annually or less —during the action learning set. The company's present annual turnover rate stands at 29 percent. The national annual turnover rate is 18 percent, and in the community where Poindexter operates, turnover averages 16 percent annually across all industries and occupations.

During the first few meetings, the team members brainstormed possible solutions to reduce employee turnover rates. They conducted research, analyzed data, and developed several ideas they thought could work.

Experimenting with Solutions

The team experimented with several solutions to cut the employee turnover rate. Each team member assumed responsibility for one solution to test. The team members were encouraged to take risks and learn from their mistakes. The team leader held regular meetings to compare notes on experiments and keep the team brainstorming on solutions. The team facilitator met individually with team members and sat in on meetings to help team members work together more effectively.

Placing Equal Emphasis on Business Results and Individual Development

The team was focused on achieving measurable business results to reduce turnover rate. But there was also an equal emphasis placed on individual and team development. Each team member was given specific tasks that aligned with his or her strengths and development needs. The team members were encouraged to support each other, share experiences, and learn from each other. That was even more important because the team members represented different functional areas of the company, different levels on the organization chart, and a diversity of cultural backgrounds.

Reaching Completion of the Action Learning Set

After several weeks of experimenting with solutions, the team members met to evaluate their progress. They realized that some experiments simply did not work, while others showed promise. They focused on the solutions that showed promise, to improve them.

Eventually, the team experimented with longevity bonuses (giving people money for staying with the company), engagement surveys to identify problems that resulted in resignations so that decisive action could be taken on them, and interpersonal skills training and coaching for all executives, managers, and supervisors in the company.

Debriefing the Action Learning Team Members Collectively

The team members were collectively debriefed by the team facilitator on their progress and shared their experiences. They discussed what worked, what did not work, and what they had learned during the action learning set. They also discussed how they could improve their solutions and implement them in the company.

Debriefing the Action Learning Team Members Individually

Each team member was debriefed individually by the team facilitator to discuss his or her personal development during the action learning set. Each team member was given feedback on his or her strengths, areas for improvement, and how the lessons gained from the team experience could be applied to their jobs.

Reassigning Action Learning Team Members

Based on the debriefing, the team members were reassigned to different action learning sets that aligned with their individual development needs. This helped them to apply their learning and continue to develop their skills in their job roles. Some of their action learning projects required full-time participation; other projects were conducted part-time while the team members shouldered the responsibilities of their regular job duties. But no matter whether the project was conducted full-time or part-time, each member of an action learning team was evaluated on the action learning set in his or her annual performance review.

The action learning set succeeded in reducing employee turnover rates in the manufacturing company. The team members experimented with solutions, learned from their mistakes, and implemented effective solutions. The focus on individual development helped the team members to improve their skills and apply their learning in their job roles. The action learning set was a valuable experience for both the team members and the company.

Case Story Conclusion

The action learning set succeeded in reducing employee turnover rates in the manufacturing company as well as developing team members through on-the-job work experience. The team members experimented with solutions, learned from their mistakes, and implemented effective solutions. The focus on team and individual development helped the team members to improve their skills and apply their learning in their job roles. The action learning set was a valuable experience for both the team members and the company.

Accelerating the Learning Process in the Action Learning Program

The action learning program described in the case study involved a process that spanned several weeks. In some cases, it may be necessary to accelerate the learning process due to time constraints or urgency. Here are ways the learning process in the case study could be organized better and carried out faster:

1. *Use Technology.* Technology can accelerate the learning process in the action learning program. For instance, virtual meeting platforms can hold virtual meetings, reducing the need for physical meetings. Additionally, online learning platforms can deliver microlearning modules and other learning materials, allowing team members to learn at their own pace.
2. *Reduce the Size of the Team.* The action learning team consisted of six members. In some cases, a smaller team size may be necessary to accelerate the learning process. A smaller team size can help to improve communication, reduce coordination efforts, and make decision-making faster.
3. *Increase the Frequency of Meetings.* To accelerate the learning process, the frequency of meetings could be increased. Instead of meeting once a week, the team could meet twice or three times a week. This would provide more opportunities for team members to share their experiences, learn from each other, and make progress.
4. *Increase the Intensity of the Learning Experience.* The learning experience in the action learning program could be made more intense to accelerate the learning process. For instance, team members could be given more challenging tasks, asked to complete them within shorter timeframes, and be held accountable for their results. This would help

to create a sense of urgency, foster a culture of innovation and experimentation, and accelerate learning.

5. *Use a Pre-Structured Learning Path.* The learning process in the action learning program could be organized and carried out faster by using a pre-structured learning path. This would involve creating a step-by-step process for the team to follow, with specific tasks, deadlines, and learning objectives. This would help to ensure that the learning process is organized, efficient, and effective.

Making Accelerated Action Learning Teams Self-Organizing

For AAL teams to become self-organizing, management must function as an enabler. Even if management acts as an enabler, authors believe that, generally, it will be a matter of the "level of awareness, preparedness, and willingness" of the organizational members. This means that they have been exposed to AAL in the past and how comfortable they have become in using it. Have they realized the external and internal benefits of operating as an AAL team member? External benefits like becoming more visible and more effective will be discussed in the later chapters. Internal benefits include increased levels of self-confidence and self-esteem. Self-organizing teams increase participation, emotional attachment to the organization, commitment, motivation, and responsibility (Moe et al., 2008). Also, these teams have decision-making authority so that it improves the speed and accuracy of problem-solving (Tata and Prasad, 2004). These teams fit well with action learning, which aims at real-time problem-solving and real-time learning in organizations. If these outcomes have been realized, employees will be self-motivated to join such teams and volunteer to form self-organizing teams.

Also, let us look at how management becomes or acts as an enabler. An organization's managers can:

■ Recognize and/or reward the employees who identify gaps and issue(s)
■ Encourage discussion among process functions
■ Give access to information
■ Create platforms for discussion on the outcomes.

Accelerated Action Learning (AAL) and Talent Deployment

The COVID-19 pandemic has changed the way we work. Recent studies have shown that 56 percent of all US jobs could be done in whole or in part from home, and 39 percent of workers have indicated in surveys that they would take a pay cut if they could work from home without need to go to a central office. Where there is a talent shortage globally, employers must grow more creative in how they acquire, develop, and retain talent.

One way for employers to become more creative is to explore applications of AAL and issues like talent deployment. But what is talent deployment? And how might AAL and talent deployment help in talent acquisition and talent retention?

Although development is an important issue for AAL, it can also help to address another business issue—that is, talent deployment. Talent deployment is not so much about acquiring talent, developing talent, engaging talent, or retaining talent as it is about making sure that people remain suitable and intellectually/emotionally fresh in their jobs. *Talent deployment* means "ensuring that the right people are kept in the right places."

Think about it. How long should people continue doing the same jobs? How do we know we still have the right person for the job over time? If we have a worker or a manager in the same job for 30 years, is that a good or a bad thing? Who monitors the time in a position in your organization? How long should people stay in the same jobs without new challenges? (Some multinational companies have a rule that each worker should be given a major job change or challenge every four to seven years.)

What are typical steps in a talent deployment effort? The steps may be to:

■ Establish policies and procedures governing how long people should remain in the same job
■ Identify present jobs in the organization and the individuals in those jobs
■ Monitor how long people are in the same job
■ Monitor the challenges people are given in their jobs
■ Determine what to do to give people fresh deployment challenges
■ Communicate information about deployment issues in talent development review meetings or otherwise bring deployment issues to the attention of workers' immediate supervisors

- Try to implement deployment efforts—such as job rotations or AAL sets
- Evaluate, periodically, the impact of talent deployment efforts on individuals and on the organization.

Talent deployment can be related to AAL. AAL can give managers and workers fresh challenges. It can keep them engaged and give them opportunities to establish cross-functional and cross-cultural social networks.

Talent deployment is important because it ensures that workers are given fresh challenges. Because many young workers consider work challenges as an important way for them to keep their skills current and thus ensure their continued employability, talent deployment efforts should be part of any robust talent management and development program.

Identifying and Overcoming Barriers to Accelerated Action Learning

Accelerated action learning is not appropriate for all organizations. Barriers exist. This section focuses on identifying and overcoming barriers to AAL.

Barriers to Accelerated Action Learning

- Managers may not support the approach
- Managers may prefer other ways to accomplish work results and develop people
- Workers may not feel comfortable working on action learning teams and may not be willing to assume responsibility for solving problems
- Workers may rebel against the stress that results from performing under pressure
- Managers may reject the solutions that workers find to problems, the training approach(es) that workers propose to meet training needs, the vision that workers formulate, or the way goals are achieved
- Managers may have trouble "letting go" and allowing workers to experiment with solutions, preferring the power trip they experience from micromanaging.

Other barriers may be experienced when trying to implement accelerated action learning.

The first barrier to applying accelerated action learning is *lack of awareness*. Decision-makers and/or workers may be reluctant to use AAL simply because they have never heard of it. If they have, they have thoughts about whether it will jeopardize the quality of the outcome because of increased focus on time management, as they may need more experience with AAL.

A second barrier to applying AAL is that *decision-makers possess single-minded views about when, where, and how people learn best*. Thus, the preferences and values of the decision-makers about when, where, and how people learn best are essential. If, for instance, decision-makers would rather send workers to off-the-job training rather than encourage them to assume full responsibility for their on-the-job learning experiences, then that will constitute a barrier to AAL.

A third barrier to applying AAL is *vested interests*. For instance, if trainers or instructional designers prefer to assume responsibility for any steps in training design, alternative approaches, that rely in whole or part on employee/learner involvement, will encounter a barrier. Similarly, trainers or instructional designers need to possess the skills to facilitate AAL projects so they can apply AAL.

There may be other reasons traditional or accelerated action learning will not work in your organization. In the case of AAL, since microlearning, nano learning, and interaction through virtual modes are a few of the most critical elements, lack of access to digital platforms, mobile platforms and laptops, and online meeting apps can be potential barriers. In each case, vested interest may exist to use other approaches.

It is worth noting one final barrier. The authors have found that, when using action learning, the approach can fail if workers are not held accountable for their performance in an action learning set. If workers are given key performance indicators (KPIs) for their on-the-job performance but no such KPIs are established for performance on action learning sets, then workers will do what they are rewarded for doing and will be less than enthusiastic about doing what they are not rewarded for doing.

Overcoming Barriers to Accelerated Action Learning

To address the *lack of awareness,* someone (usually a team facilitator) should take up the cause of building awareness about AAL. This can be done by:

- Circulating articles or books (such as this one) about AAL
- Preparing white papers for key decision-makers to describe action learning and show how it may be applied to addressing organizational problems, issues, goals, or challenges (use the FAQ in the Appendix at the end of this book)
- Offering voluntary briefing sessions—such as brown bag lunches—to workers and managers about AAL to build their awareness of what it is
- Experimenting with AAL or pilot testing it with existing committees, groups, teams, or task forces already in operation within the organization (use the simulation at the end of this book).

To eliminate the barrier caused by *single-minded views about where and how people learn best*, champions of action learning are well advised to *demonstrate other ways*. One way to do that is to undertake small-scale pilot tests of AAL in the organization with the support of open-minded managers to demonstrate its value.

Suppose trainers or instructional designers are concerned that they must possess the competencies to support AAL. In that case, they may be trained to build those competencies. To eliminate the barrier created by vested interests, champions of AAL should challenge those vested interests to experiment with new approaches, perhaps designing a field experiment of AAL to demonstrate what it is and what demonstrable benefits may stem from applying it.

Two Approaches to Experimentation in Accelerated Action Learning: The Analytical Approach and the Creative Approach

An Action Learning team uses two typical approaches: the analytical approach and the creative approach.

The Analytical Approach

The *analytical approach* is directed toward finding a logical solution to a problem. It is used when team members decide that the correct question to ask is this: *What is the most logical way to identify and solve a problem?* When team members use the analytical approach, they follow the typical steps in problem-solving (Rothwell, 1999):

- *Step 1*: Define the problem or issue
- *Step 2*: Investigate the problem or issue
- *Step 3*: Isolate cause(s) of the problem or variables affecting the issue
- *Step 4*: Propose solution(s) to address the problem or issue
- *Step 5*: Experiment with solutions to the problems or issue
- *Step 6*: Modify the solution(s) based on experience
- *Step 7*: Try out new solutions
- *Step 8*: Draw conclusions based on the investigation and the experiment and report those to interested stakeholders.

These steps guide the efforts of the Action Learning team, providing a road-map for what to do. See Exhibit 12.1 for a tool to help apply this approach.

Exhibit 12.1 A Worksheet for Planning an Accelerated Action Learning Project Using the Analytical Approach

Directions: Use this worksheet to help team members plan a project. For each question, make notes or comments about what the team needs to do or has already done to answer the question. Use the questions and answers as a starting point to plan the action learning project.

	Has the Action Learning Team:
1	*Defined the problem or issue?*
2	*Investigated the problem or issue?*
3	*Isolated cause(s) of the problem or variables affecting the issue?*
4	*Proposed solution(s) to address the problem or issue?*
5	*Experimented with solution(s) to the problem or issue?*
6	*Modified the solution(s) based on experience?*

7	*Tried out new solution(s) with a time limit?*
8	*Had a reflection based on the investigation and the experiment and reported those to interested stakeholders?*

The Creative Approach

The *creative approach* is directed toward finding a new definition of a problem or issue—a process called *reframing*—and is intended to prompt breakthroughs. It is used when team members decide that the correct question to ask is: *"Is there a more creative way to define or solve a problem than the most obvious one?"* When team members use the creative approach, they follow the typical steps (Rothwell, 1999):

- *Step 1*: Gather information about the problem or issue
- *Step 2*: Apply various creativity-enhancing techniques to the problem or issue
- *Step 3*: Reach new conclusions about the definition of the problem or issue
- *Step 4*: Propose solution(s) to address the problem or issue as it has been creatively reframed
- *Step 5*: Apply various creativity-enhancing techniques to the solution or issue
- *Step 6*: Reach new conclusions about the solution or issue
- *Step 7*: Experiment with the creatively reframed solutions to see whether they work
- *Step 8*: Modify the solution(s) based on experience
- *Step 9*: Try out new solutions
- *Step 10*: Draw conclusions based on the investigation and the experiment, and report those to interested stakeholders.

These steps can guide the efforts of the Accelerated Action Learning team and provide a roadmap for team action. Many creativity-enhancing techniques can be applied as an Accelerated Action Learning team investigates problems, issues, opportunities, goals, or solutions. See Exhibit 12.2 for a tool to help apply this approach.

Exhibit 12.2 A Worksheet for Planning an Accelerated Action Learning Project Using the Creative Approach

	Directions: Use this worksheet to help team members plan a project. For each question, make notes or comments about what the team needs to do or has done to answer the question. Use the questions and answers as a starting point to plan the action learning project.
	Has the Accelerated Action Learning Team:
1	Learned about the audience for the results of the action learning team? By observation and interview, does the team know who is the final user of the team's results and why that person or group cares about it?
2	Answered the following questions: What is the problem? What are the needs? Why is this important? Does this problem matter?
3	Generated many creative solutions?
4	Answered the following question: How can we show our team's ideas?
5	Tested the prototype? What worked? What did not?
6	Held a reflection session on what team members learned from experimentation?

Time Frames

It is common to think that action learning requires long periods to carry out. However, that is not always the case. The time frame that is required depends on the scope and complexity of the issue the team is addressing. It is thus possible to carry out an *action learning set*—that is, an action learning experience—in a staff meeting, training course, or over a lunch hour.

Action learning is often integrated into training experiences and thus gets accelerated naturally. In those cases, participants in training are broken up into teams to apply the principles they have learned to a work-related problem. Such action learning teams are often of short duration—such as 45 minutes to several days.

Settings

Where do accelerated action learning teams meet? Again, the tendency is to think of these experiences as carried out in off-the-job meetings or in lengthy off-the-job retreats. But that is not required. It all depends on the scope and complexity of the issue that the team has been charged to address. It is possible for an accelerated action learning team to meet over the lunch table, at dinner, at the water cooler, or next to someone's desk.

Team Member Roles

Team members may be given—or may adopt—different roles during AAL experiences. Typical roles might include team leader, team secretary or scribe, team messenger, and team timekeeper. The *team leader* exerts influence over others to keep the team on task and to coordinate team efforts. The *team secretary* prepares the agenda for meetings, keeps and distributes minutes of team meetings, and types up written material for the team. The *team messenger* may visit managers or other stakeholders on behalf of the team to collect information. The *team timekeeper* ensures that the team allocates time to tasks and to meetings. Other team roles may be added, as necessary. If a team breaks up into smaller groups to focus on specific tasks, then new roles may need to be added for each small group.

The Team Leader's Role

The team leader role is familiar to many people who work in project formats. Team leaders are essentially project leaders, working to ensure that the team meets deadlines and works on or under budget. The competencies of team leaders are described well by various project management programs (Cartwright and Yinger, 2007). The team leader assists the AAL group in setting specific goals and objectives and checks whether those have been achieved during the AAL process.

The Team Facilitator's Role

Team facilitators enact a role different from all others. Facilitators help team members work together effectively. Facilitators focus their attention on group process rather than on group tasks. They may periodically raise such questions as these:

- How do we feel we are working together?
- How could this meeting have been improved?
- What has the team learned?
- What could we do to work together more effectively?

Team facilitators may periodically ask team members to individually complete a questionnaire about the team's work processes. He or she then may use that to focus team attention on areas for improvement.

Common Mistakes or Problems in AAL Teams

Several mistakes or problems are common in AAL teams, as they are in other small groups. They include:

- Aggressive or dominating behavior by one or more team members
- Withdrawal or inaction by one or more team members
- Disruptive behavior.

The team facilitator's role is to monitor group process. The team facilitator's role includes responsibility to intervene when the behavior of individual team members impedes team process.

Team facilitators may rely on three general approaches to address common group problems. *Applying skillful questions* is one approach. When one team member becomes too aggressive, for instance, then the team facilitator intervenes to ask other team members for their opinion. If no opinion is offered, then the team facilitator may offer his or her own opinion. *Calling a "time out"* is a second approach that team facilitators may use. A "time out" is a signal to focus on group process, the "how" of group interaction.

By doing that, team facilitators draw attention to behavior that impedes group process. *Talking to individuals outside of the group setting* is a third approach. Team facilitators may call a break and speak to one person. That person can then be tactfully confronted with what he or she is doing, how that differs from team ground rules or expectations, what consequences his or her behavior is having on the group, and what he or she should do to rectify the problem that he or she is causing. Team facilitators should take special care when confronting an individual about his or her behavior, since the goal is not to cause hard feelings or produce a chilling effect on group interaction but (instead) to improve group interaction. If the individual is silent after being confronted, he or she should be gently drawn out and encouraged by the team facilitator, who should praise behaviors to the team when demonstrated.

Example

An AAL team was assembled to investigate and correct a production bottle-neck during paperwork processing in a life insurance company. Team members were selected cross-functionally. Each member represented each work unit that received an insurance application for processing. At the outset, each member had a positive attitude about the AAL process, on which they had been briefed, and about other team members.

The team facilitator was chosen from the Human Resources Department and was exceptionally skilled in group facilitation methods and in project management.

After team members were oriented to AAL and to the problem they were to investigate, they planned their project around the typical steps in problem-solving. The team facilitator introduced them to the steps and posed these questions:

- *Step 1*: What is the problem?
- *Step 2*: How can the problem be investigated?
- *Step 3*: How can the cause(s) of the problem be isolated?
- *Step 4*: What possible solution(s) can help to solve the problem?
- *Step 5*: How can the team experiment with solution(s) to the problem?
- *Step 6*: How can the solution(s) be effectively modified based on experience?

- *Step 7*: How can the team organize and try out more effective solution(s) based on their experience?
- *Step 8*: What conclusions can be based on the investigation and the experiment, and how can the results be reported to interested stakeholders?

The team then elected a leader, a secretary, and a timekeeper. The team began by flowcharting the work process, checking what they believed to be the steps in processing a new insurance application against the understanding of supervisors in each unit where new applications were processed. By the end of the investigation, a flowchart had been constructed that showed the steps of processing a new application and the time required for each step. By this point, applications encountered a bottleneck in the Underwriting Department when physicians were queried for information about the prospective policy owner. Although most of the process flowed smoothly until that point, the duration of the policy issue process roughly doubled when physicians were asked for information.

Once the source of the problem was pinpointed, the team members brainstormed on ways to slash the time needed to receive information from physicians. They included members of the Underwriting Department in that process. Possible solutions included:

- Providing queries by e-mail or fax, rather than by letter
- Providing an incentive for physicians who responded quickly
- Restructuring the information requested to make it easy for a physician to respond to it.

Telephone interviews were held with physicians, too, to gain their perspective and their opinions about the cause(s) of the problem and the most effective solutions. Team members also benchmarked the approaches used at other insurance companies to deal with the same problem.

The team members then experimented with each solution alone and in combination.

The elapsed time between request and answer was monitored for each solution individually and collectively. The results revealed that "restructuring the information requested" was most effective in slashing the processing time. That solution was tried again—with an even more streamlined form.

The result was a dramatic reduction in the processing time of life insurance applications.

Everyone benefited from this application of AAL. The company benefited by eliminating a bottleneck. All team members benefited by learning more about the application process and about how each work unit processed applications. Individual team members built competencies in work process analysis, flow-charting, benchmarking, and problem-solving. Physicians benefited because demands on their time for insurance applications were dramatically reduced.

How Can an AAL Team Experiment With Solutions?

AAL teams are usually empowered to experiment with solutions to the problems they are trying to solve or to the issues they are trying to address. This section describes the most common ways to experiment with solutions, summarizes the most common mistakes made during experimentation and recommends ways to avoid them, and provides an example of what happens when an AAL team experiments with solutions.

There are four common approaches to experimenting with solutions to problems.

Developing a Prototype

Developing a prototype is a first approach to experimenting with solutions. A *prototype* is defined as a model of what a solution will look like. Prototypes are usually thought of as tangible—such as a piece of equipment. But pro-totypes may also be intangible, such as a drawing that represents a new approach to a work process or to a service delivery method. A prototype may only be partially implemented, but it should demonstrate the basic functionality of the solution. Prototypes are valuable because they permit real-world experimentation. *Rapid prototyping* permits teams to experiment quickly with many possible solutions.

Developing Written Scenarios

Developing written scenarios is a second approach to experimenting with solutions. A *scenario* is a description of what is likely to happen in a hypo-thetical situation. Scenarios are usually presented as an answer to a "What if this happens?" situation.

Creating Simulations

Creating simulations is a third approach to experimenting with solutions. A simulation can be manual or electronic. A *manual simulation* places a prospective performer into an artificial situation based on research about real situations. Workers then experience the simulation, and members of an AAL team review the results.

To cite a simple example of a manual simulation, suppose that an AAL team is experimenting with a new manufacturing flow on an assembly line. Nobody is sure how it will work. It looks good on paper. The AAL team sets up an assembly line away from the actual work setting to simulate how the new assembly line flow would operate. The members then monitor results against the actual results being achieved. If the simulation indicates that the simulated approach is likely to produce cost savings, quality improvement, or increased productivity, then it may be implemented on an actual assembly line.

An electronic simulation is computerized. Workers are guided through a computer-based situation meant to be like what they might experience in reality. Action team members then review the results to see how workers performed in the simulated setting.

Conducting Pilot Tests

Conducting pilot tests is a fourth approach to experimenting with solutions. A *pilot test* is a small-scale test of a new approach carried out under real-world conditions. A company that wants to implement team-based management, for instance, might select one work unit to be a pilot test for team-based management. Pilot tests may be set up to "test reality"—or to provide compelling evidence of the value of a new approach.

Common Mistakes or Problems in Accelerated Action Learning

AAL teams are prone to several common mistakes or problems as they experiment with solutions. Among these mistakes or problems are:

- *Red herrings*: Getting sidetracked by issues not really related to the problem or issue being investigated.

- *Listening to "warm fuzzies"*: Failing to be clear about the specific issue or problem being solved.
- *Jumping to conclusions*: Leaping to an answer based on limited facts or examples.
- *Becoming embroiled in organizational politics*: Seizing on a solution because the right people want it for their own reasons or to meet their own agenda.
- *The halo effect*: Viewing a solution as positive while overlooking possible negative side effects.
- *The horn effect*: Viewing a solution as negative while overlooking possible positive side effects.
- *The central tendency error*: An over-eagerness to compromise by "splitting the difference" on solutions or by averaging results.
- *The* vox populi *error*: Favoring a solution because "everyone likes it" rather than favoring the solution because it is the best, the most practical, or the optimal approach.

To address these problems or mistakes, team members should ask themselves at least two key questions. First and foremost is this question: *"Does the solution address the cause of the problem rather than symptoms or side effects?"* By focusing on that question, team members should be able to avoid the most common mistakes or problems made in solving problems. Second is this question: *Does the solution produce a genuine, measurable improvement?"* Can the team document a *measurable* improvement from the experiment they conducted.

Example

An AAL team was assembled to improve the manufacturing flow on an assembly line in a manufacturing firm. Team members were selected to experiment with various manufacturing flows to find the most efficient one. The team developed a flowchart that would result in the most efficient manufacturing flow. They pilot-tested it by setting up an actual assembly line and trying it out. The results revealed that, as they suspected, the new flowchart prompted a much more efficient production line. Team members documented the results that were measurable.

Kolb's Learning Cycle and Accelerated Action Learning

It's intriguing to study how people learn. It includes a broad variety of cognitive processes. Over the past few decades, a range of, oftentimes contradicting, theoretical concepts have been used to explain this somewhat cryptic and concealed behavior. Experiential Learning Theory (ELT), one of the most significant frameworks, was proposed by David Kolb in 1984 (Kolb, 1984). It is one of the most widely used models of learning styles. ELT is based on the notion that experiential or hands-on learning is the most effective way for individuals to learn.

Learning facilitation strategies change over time. But now that a new trend, toward evidence-based practice, has emerged, informed by the most recent findings on brain structure and brain chemistry, we are better able to choose instructional tactics that will probably have a positive impact on learning.

Having a solid model for how knowledge is formed from experience is essential for improving learner success.

Traditionally, experiential learning has been incorporated into school along with internships or job-shadowing experiences.

The essential themes of Kolb's theory are the learner's growth and perspective. Experiential learning lays greater responsibility on learners to guide their own learning than the traditional, didactic approach does. Experiential learning is a great form of learning because it helps learners to apply their knowledge in real-world situations. Experiential learning promotes active participation, critical thinking, creativity, problem-solving, cooperation, and communication skills. Additionally, they fit with accelerated action learning.

Traditional approaches to instruction often rely on time-honored approaches such as homework, lectures, and textbooks. Despite the fact that facts and concepts are taught using these techniques, it is not always obvious how to apply them in work settings.

Even though these two teaching approaches achieve different goals, there is no doubt that experiential learning is preferred for helping students remember information.

Instructors frequently use Kolb's Learning Cycle, whether they know it or not. The approach outlined below exemplifies this procedure (Kolb, 1984):

1. *Orientation*: Through experience (in the actual world) and reflection, learners become familiar with the topic.
2. *Cognitive Processing*: Through practical exercises, learners actively engage with the topic.
3. *Retrieval*: Through repetition and memory, learners recollect the material.
4. *Consolidation*: The process by which learners commit new knowledge to long-term memory.
5. *Motivation and Evaluation*: Learners assess the value of the activity.
6. *Integration*: Learners combine new knowledge with what they already know.
7. *Application*: Learners use the new knowledge to address issues.
8. *Exploration*: Learners keep researching the subject.

Consider how these steps might relate to the steps of accelerated action learning.

Defining the Four Stages of Kolb's Learning Cycle

David Kolb contends that a person's life experiences, heredity, and the needs of the modern world all have an impact on the preferred methods of learning. The spiral of immediate experience that a learner climbs leads to reflections and observations of the experience, according to David Kolb. The theories or abstract notions that are created from these reflections, after they have been integrated with past information, assimilation, and transformation, lead to novel behaviors and ways of reacting to the experience that may be explored and tested. The Kolb Learning Cycle was developed by David Kolb as a method or model of human learning. He used this approach to train his pupils at Stanford University. Through individual research, he hoped to increase their understanding.

Kolb recognized four primary learning styles, in addition to developing a learning style survey and an experiential learning theory. The internal cognitive processes of learners are a major focus of Kolb's theory. The two tiers of his experiential learning theory include his four experience learning cycles and four learning styles. Learning, according to Kolb, is the acquisition of abstract experience that may be used flexibly in a variety of circumstances. According to Kolb's educational theory, the experiential approach acts as a catalyst for the development of new ideas and conceptions.

The stages of Kolb's experiential learning cycle are (Kolb, 1984):

1. *Concrete Experience*: The learner exhibits personal interaction with others in everyday situations. In work environments, learners generally depend less on a rigorous approach to problem-solving but rely more on emotions, openness to new ideas, and flexibility.
2. *Reflective Observation*: At this point, learners are able to comprehend situations and ideas from several angles. They rely on endurance, objectivity, and judgment, yet take no action. The opinions of learners are based on their feelings and thoughts.
3. *Abstract Conceptualization*: At this point, rather than relying on interpersonal concerns or emotions, learners use concepts, logical methods, and theories to understand situations or dilemmas. To deal with problems in the actual world, they frequently rely on structured planning and theories and concepts.
4. *Active Experimentation*: The learners demonstrate active learning during this stage by experimenting with numerous scenarios. During the active experimental stage, the learners take a practical approach, rather than just observe a situation.

The four-stage process of concrete experience, observation, reflection, and generalization aids in forming the abstract concept (logical analysis) and generalizations (conclusions), which are applied for testing in subsequent situations. They lead to new experiences as the foundation for effective learning. In contrast to "classroom-confined" methods, this approach allows the development of genuine problem-solving challenges.

The cycle of experiential learning may be used to teach students in a variety of contexts. By introducing learners to this learning strategy, team facilitators can motivate them to develop their problem-solving skills. The learning cycle can help students more quickly and thoroughly understand concepts and ideas.

Team facilitators guide students through the learning cycle, providing them with an opportunity to practice their critical thinking skills and open their minds to new ideas. Team facilitators can use the learning cycles to instruct students in a variety of disciplines. For example, if an instructor wished to teach learners about the concept of time, he or she might begin by asking them to think about their personal interactions with time. The learners might be told to keep track of time at that point by the instructor. The instructor can next ask the students to critically assess the time. Finally, the instructor might ask learners for possible time management techniques.

What Do Kolb's Four Learning Dimensions Mean?

When one is aware of another person's (or one's own) learning preferences, the learning experience can be focused on the selected strategy. The idea is to apply the emphasis that works best for the situation at hand and the individual's learning preferences. Everyone reacts to and requires stimulation of all learning types to varied degrees.

The four learning components identified by Kolb help create a learning environment that improves people's capabilities and all-around skill sets. By integrating these four components, Kolb develops the following four comprehensive learning dimensions (Kolb, 1984):

1. *Diverging*: These people utilize their imagination to learn in a creative way and have a range of points of view. Divergent learners learn best via real experience and careful observation, preferring to observe rather than act.
2. *Assimilating*: They are skilled in exploring and delving into learning style models. They are more engaged in technological activities having a logical structure and a conceptual framework. Their main characteristics are reflective observation and abstract conceptualization.
3. *Converging*: They are considered to be good problem-solvers and realistic in their analytical approach to tasks and concepts. They tend to converge on their intended solutions and are characterized by active exploration and abstract conceptualization.
4. *Accommodating*: They learn more pragmatically and often take an intuitive approach to problems. These people could rely heavily on their instincts. Active experimentation, concrete learning, and a love of challenges make up the majority of their characteristics.

How Kolb's Instructional Methods Can Be Integrated with Accelerated Action Learning

What are the effects of Kolb's Learning Cycle on instruction in any setting—including AAL sets?

The four learning cycles and learning dimensions can adapt learning methods by AAL teams.

Consider:

1. It enables team facilitators to concentrate more on specific learning goals for learners.

2. It makes it feasible to create coaching activities, teaching methods, and training sessions that help a lifelong learner in understanding the subject matter in formal learning settings.
3. Team facilitators can utilize the four stages of Kolb's experiential learning cycle to tailor any educational strategy or intervention for learners.

By providing certain specific learning style efforts and educational techniques, team facilitators can boost the possibility that adult learners on teams will successfully absorb the learning and can develop ideas they would not have considered if the learning were performed in a different style. The chosen learning preferences of their learners can be ascertained by the team facilitators. Giving learners engaging learning opportunities is a good idea. Team facilitators can help learners become more flexible and adaptable by doing this.

All levels of learning, in Kolb's view, contribute to the process of experiential learning. Learning in a classroom, for instance, could be, for learners, an abstract experience, but it can also turn into a concrete experience if, for instance, learners emulate and look up to the team facilitator.

References

Cartwright, C., & Yinger, M. (2007). *Project management competency development framework—Second edition.* Paper presented at PMI® Global Congress 2007—EMEA, Budapest, Hungary, Newtown Square, PA: Project Management Institute.

Kolb, D. (1984). *Experiential learning: Experience as the source of learning and development.* Prentice-Hall.

Moe, N. B., Dingsøyr, T., & Dybå, T. (2008, March). Understanding self-organizing teams in agile software development. *Proceedings of the 19th Australian Conference on Software Engineering, Australia,* 76–85. https://doi.org/10.1109/ASWEC.2008.4483195

Rothwell, W. J. (1999). *The action learning guidebook: A real-time strategy for problem solving, training design, and employee development.* Pfeiffer.

Tata, J., & Prasad, S. (2004). Team self-management, organizational structure, and judgments of team effectiveness. *Journal of Managerial Issues, 16*(2), 248–265.

Appendix I

An Assessment Instrument for Accelerated Action Learning Facilitators

Background

Competency assessment identifies what characteristics lead to successful performance for individuals in organizational settings. Competency assessment can be a starting point for establishing strategic development plans linked to organizational strategy and individual development needs.

Use this instrument to identify the accelerated action learning facilitation competencies critical to your organization's success and assess your current competence.

As you complete each competency category on the instrument, compile a subtotal for the center and right-hand columns and place the score in the appropriate box on each page. When you finish the entire instrument, copy your scores from each box to the appropriate totals at the end of the instrument.

Assessment Instrument for Accelerated Action Learning Facilitators

Directions: Reflect on your ability to demonstrate these competencies. First, rate how well you demonstrate each competency by *circling* the appropriate number under "Current Competence." Use these definitions to help you identify your level of current competence:

- *Basic* means you have a fundamental understanding of the competency/task and can explain it to others
- *Intermediate* means you can demonstrate the competency/task but may still require development in demonstrating it effectively
- *Advanced* means you can demonstrate the competency/task and require no development because you feel you are most effective in demonstrating that competency/task.

Then, identify which competencies/tasks are necessary for your current or future work success.

Competency/Task	Current Competence							Is This Task Necessary for Current or Future Work Success?	
	None	*Basic*		*Intermediate*	*Advanced*			*Current Work* ⊠	*Future Work* ⊠
Using Body Language									
1. I use effective eye contact	0	1	2	3	4	5	6	☐	☐
2. I lean forward to pay attention to others	0	1	2	3	4	5	6	☐	☐
Total Score:									
Listening Actively									
3. I pay careful attention to other people as they speak	0	1	2	3	4	5	6	☐	☐
4. I listen effectively to the content of messages	0	1	2	3	4	5	6	☐	☐
5. I listen effectively to the feelings underlying what others say	0	1	2	3	4	5	6	☐	☐
Total Score:									

Competency/Task	Current Competence							Is This Task Necessary for Current or Future Work Success?	
	None	Basic		Intermediate		Advanced		Current Work ☒	Future Work ☒
Paraphrasing Thought and Feeling									
6. With small group participants, I repeat the content of short segments of what they say	0	1	2	3	4	5	6	☐	☐
7. With small group participants, I repeat the feelings in short segments of what they say	0	1	2	3	4	5	6	☐	☐
Total Score:									
Summarizing Thought and Feeling									
8. I repeat to small group participants the content of longer segments of what they say	0	1	2	3	4	5	6	☐	☐
9. I repeat to small group participants the feelings in longer segments of what they say	0	1	2	3	4	5	6	☐	☐
Total Score:									
Observing Body Language and Small Group Dynamics									
10. I watch individuals effectively, noting any indications of how they feel about the facilitator or other participants in the small group	0	1	2	3	4	5	6	☐	☐

Competency/Task	Current Competence							Is This Task Necessary for Current or Future Work Success?	
	None	Basic		Intermediate		Advanced		Current Work ☒	Future Work ☒
11. I watch individuals effectively, noting any indications of how they feel about what is said by other participants in a small group or by me	0	1	2	3	4	5	6	☐	☐
12. I watch groups effectively, detecting the level of group interest and energy	0	1	2	3	4	5	6	☐	☐
13. I match my behaviors with group dynamics	0	1	2	3	4	5	6	☐	☐
14. I demonstrate familiarity with facilitator roles in the *forming stage* of group development	0	1	2	3	4	5	6	☐	☐
15. I demonstrate familiarity with facilitator roles in the *storming stage* of group development	0	1	2	3	4	5	6	☐	☐
16. I demonstrate familiarity with facilitator roles in the *norming stage* of group development	0	1	2	3	4	5	6	☐	☐
17. I demonstrate familiarity with facilitator roles in the *performing stage* of group development	0	1	2	3	4	5	6	☐	☐
Total Score:									

Competency/Task	Current Competence							Is This Task Necessary for Current or Future Work Success?	
	None	Basic		Intermediate		Advanced		Current Work ⊠	Future Work ⊠
Applying Skillful Questions									
18. I know how to use closed questions	0	1	2	3	4	5	6	☐	☐
19. I know how to use open questions	0	1	2	3	4	5	6	☐	☐
20. I can demonstrate the ability to use open and closed questions *with individuals*	0	1	2	3	4	5	6	☐	☐
21. I can demonstrate the ability to use open and closed questions *with groups*	0	1	2	3	4	5	6	☐	☐
Total Score:									
Expressing the Facilitator's Ideas and Feelings									
22. I disclose what I *think* about ideas raised *by individuals*	0	1	2	3	4	5	6	☐	☐
23. I disclose what I *think* about ideas raised *by a group*	0	1	2	3	4	5	6	☐	☐
24. I disclose what I *feel* about ideas raised by *individuals* in the group	0	1	2	3	4	5	6	☐	☐
25. I disclose what I *feel* about ideas raised by *a group*	0	1	2	3	4	5	6	☐	☐
Total Score:									

Competency/Task	Current Competence						Is This Task Necessary for Current or Future Work Success?	
	None	Basic	Intermediate		Advanced		Current Work ☒	Future Work ☒
Focusing the Group's Attention								
26. I effectively emphasize key points made by *individual group members*	0	1	2	3	4	5	6	☐	☐
27. I effectively emphasize key points made by *the group*	0	1	2	3	4	5	6	☐	☐
28. I provide new information from sources external to the group	0	1	2	3	4	5	6	☐	☐
29. I draw attention to feelings expressed by *individuals in the group*	0	1	2	3	4	5	6	☐	☐
30. I draw attention to feelings expressed by the *group*	0	1	2	3	4	5	6	☐	☐
Total Score:								
Directing Group Thought								
31. I help group members establish agendas for group meetings	0	1	2	3	4	5	6	☐	☐
32. I help group members surface creative ideas from individuals in the group	0	1	2	3	4	5	6	☐	☐
33. I use the summary to direct group members' attention to important ideas	0	1	2	3	4	5	6	☐	☐

Competency/Task	Current Competence								Is This Task Necessary for Current or Future Work Success?	
	None	Basic		Intermediate		Advanced			Current Work ☒	Future Work ☒
34. I use the summary to direct group members' attention to essential feelings expressed by individuals in the group	0	1	2	3	4	5	6		☐	☐
Total Score:										
Stimulating Group Insights										
35. I help individuals discover new ideas based on group discussion	0	1	2	3	4	5	6		☐	☐
36. I help individuals discover new ideas based on individual reflection	0	1	2	3	4	5	6		☐	☐
37. I help group members discover new ideas based on group discussion	0	1	2	3	4	5	6		☐	☐
38. I help individuals discover new feelings based on group discussion	0	1	2	3	4	5	6		☐	☐
39. I help individuals discover new feelings based on individual reflection	0	1	2	3	4	5	6		☐	☐
40. I help group members discover new feelings based on group discussion	0	1	2	3	4	5	6		☐	☐
Total Score:										

INTERPRETING YOUR SCORES

If your score in these areas falls below the number stated below, then place a check mark (✓) next to the indicated score.

Competency Area	Current Competence			
Using body language and nonverbal behavior	6			
Listening actively	9			
Paraphrasing thoughts and feeling	6			
Summarizing thoughts and feeling	6			
Observing body language and small group dynamics	24			
Applying skillful questions	12			
Expressing facilitator ideas and feelings	12			
Focusing group attention	15			
Directing group thought	12			
Stimulating group insights	18			

ACTION PLANNING

Take a few moments to do some action planning. What can you do to build your competencies as a team facilitator? For each competency area, you checked above in which you need to develop yourself, list ideas for building your competencies opposite the competency area below. Do planning by discussing your development needs with peers, subordinates, supervisors, and other facilitators. There are no "right" or "wrong" answers in any absolute sense, though some answers may be better than others for developing yourself as a team facilitator.

Competency	Strategies for Building the Competency
Using body language and nonverbal behavior	
Listening actively	
Paraphrasing thoughts and feelings	
Summarizing thoughts and feelings	
Observing body language and small group dynamics	
Applying skillful questions	

Competency	Strategies for Building the Competency
Expressing facilitator ideas and feelings	
Focusing group attention	
Directing group thought	
Stimulating group insights	

Appendix II

Accelerated Action Learning Survey Results

Background

As a part of this book project, two surveys were conducted in 2022 to identify what is important in making action learning fast, virtual, and effective. Each survey targeted employees in India who had experience with action learning. Survey A was to identify the delivery method, participants, and important steps of action learning. It consists of six demographic questions and four multiple-choice questions. Survey B was to investigate the challenges and benefits of action learning and solutions for accelerated action learning. It includes six demographic questions and four open-ended questions. A summary of the overall survey results is as follows.

Survey A

Respondents

This research surveyed 36 talent development professionals in India with experience in action learning projects/sets. The respondents' organizations were separated into three industries: manufacturing (72.2 percent), other industries (22.2 percent), and transportation/communication/electric/gas (5.6 percent). Some 65.7 percent of respondents belonged to an organization with a size of 500–1999 employees, followed by 25.7 percent with 1–99 employees, 5.7 percent with 100–249 employees, and 2.9 percent with over

10,000 employees, with 2.9 percent being invalid responses. Most respondents were in the manager track position (82.4 percent). Of the respondents, 90 percent were responsible for planning the action learning projects in their organization, 90.9 percent were responsible for facilitating the action learning projects. 90.6 percent were responsible for evaluating the results of action learning projects, 77.1 percent usually facilitated action learning projects, and 77.8 percent facilitated work teams.

Results

Result 1. Virtual Action Learning

The percentage using action learning in a virtual setting varied: 0–20 percent virtual action learning (44.4 percent), 21–40 percent virtual action learning (11.1 percent), 41–60 percent virtual action learning (11.1 percent), 81–100 percent virtual action learning (25.0 percent), and 61–80 percent virtual action learning (8.3 percent).

Result 2. The Most Frequent Participants in Action Learning Projects

From the frequency of participants in action learning projects by job categories, technical employees ($M = 4.25$), supervisors ($M = 4.21$), middle

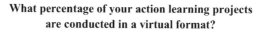

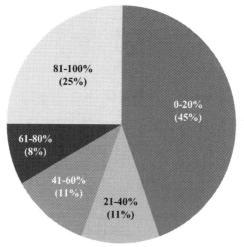

Exhibit II.1 Percentage of Action Learning Projects in Virtual Format. Note: The results shown in the figure are rounded to the nearest whole number.

managers (M = 4.09), and professional employees (M = 4.03) participated more frequently in action learning projects. Production employees (M = 3.91) and executives (M = 3.63) appeared to participate in action learning projects less frequently, while clerical employees (M = 2.50) and salespersons (M = 2.14) participated the least frequently of all job categories.

Result 3. *Importance of Action Learning Steps*

As a result of examining the importance level of the ten steps of the traditional action learning model, the results show that most steps were found to be important: identify an organization problem, goal, vision or issue (M = 4.44); select a team of people who can benefit by attacking the problem, formulating the plan, creating a vision, or addressing the issue (M = 4.36); brief the team on what is known about the problem, goal, vision, or issue (M = 4.14); provide limitations on what time, money, effort, staff, and other resources may be used to experiment to solve the problem, formulate/ achieve the goal, create the vision or address the issue (M = 4.14); encourage the group/team to experiment to solve the problem, formulate or achieve the goal, establish the vision, or address the issue (M = 4.00); identify a task

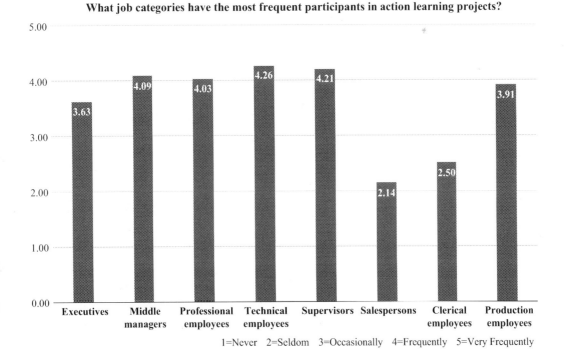

Exhibit II.2   Job Categories of the Most Frequent Participants in Action Learning Projects

leader to focus on making sure the team stays on task (*M* = 4.22); identify a team facilitator to help the team work together effectively and learn from each other (*M* = 4.03); debrief the team on what the team members collectively learned from the experience (*M* = 4.08); debrief individuals on what they learned from the experience and what they need to develop in the future (*M* = 4.06). Only one step ("reach a limitation and shut down the action learning project/set") was relatively less important than the other steps (*M* = 2.86).

Conclusion

First, the survey shows that action learning projects can be carried out in a virtual setting. The group who used virtual action learning at 21–100 percent represented over half of all respondents, compared with the case of not using virtual action learning or using a very small percentage of virtual action learning.

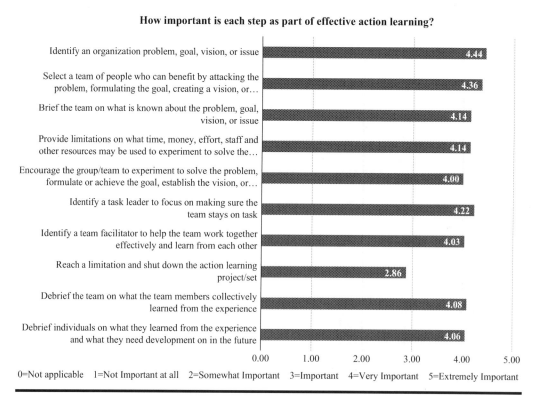

How important is each step as part of effective action learning?

Step	Value
Identify an organization problem, goal, vision, or issue	4.44
Select a team of people who can benefit by attacking the problem, formulating the goal, creating a vision, or…	4.36
Brief the team on what is known about the problem, goal, vision, or issue	4.14
Provide limitations on what time, money, effort, staff and other resources may be used to experiment to solve the…	4.14
Encourage the group/team to experiment to solve the problem, formulate or achieve the goal, establish the vision, or…	4.00
Identify a task leader to focus on making sure the team stays on task	4.22
Identify a team facilitator to help the team work together effectively and learn from each other	4.03
Reach a limitation and shut down the action learning project/set	2.86
Debrief the team on what the team members collectively learned from the experience	4.08
Debrief individuals on what they learned from the experience and what they need development on in the future	4.06

0.00   1.00   2.00   3.00   4.00   5.00

0=Not applicable   1=Not Important at all   2=Somewhat Important   3=Important   4=Very Important   5=Extremely Important

Exhibit II.3   Importance of Each Step in Action Learning

Second, from the frequency of action learning participants, various employees participated in action learning projects, but salespersons and clerical employees participated less frequently in action learning projects. It does not mean that only employees in the specific job category are invited for action learning projects. Who should attend depends on the organizational problems to be solved.

Third, each stage of action learning was identified as being important, although "reaching a limitation and shutting down the action learning project/set" was identified as being less important than the other stages. This is because, in the case of traditional action learning, when an organizational problem is solved, the project is not closed. Instead, with abundant time, action learning team members kept solving other problems or challenges related to the original problem. This naturally led to a new action learning project, so closing the action learning project might not have been a critical factor in the whole step.

Survey B

Respondents

This research surveyed 36 talent development professionals in India with experience in action learning projects/sets.

Results

Result 1. The Most Significant Problems/ Difficulties in Using Action Learning

The respondents were asked about their organization's biggest problems or difficulties in using action learning.

- Engagement
- Execution
- Internal/external communication
- Lack of buy-in (from leadership, team members, or partners)
- Lack of responsibility/ownership/commitment
- Multitasking
- Planning

- Task management
- Team management
- Teamwork
- Time management.

Result 2. The Most Significant Advantages Gained from Action Learning

The respondents were asked about the most significant advantages their organization has gained from action learning.

- Communication skills
- Confidence
- Cost and time savings
- Future readiness
- Honesty
- Insight
- Multitasking
- New knowledge and skills
- Open discussion
- Open to new ideas/solutions
- Ownership
- Positive attitude
- Problem-solving
- Proper training
- Recognition from leadership
- Self-belief
- Skill development
- Task management
- Team development/team building
- Teamwork
- Time management
- Trust
- Understanding work/work process
- Work efficiency.

Result 3. The Ways to Speed Up the Action Learning Process and How to Use it Effectively in a Virtual Setting

The respondents were asked about the ways to speed up the action learning process and also how to use it effectively in virtual settings.

- Creating a report with a specific process/writing a performance report
- Having an open discussion regularly
- Having more responsibility in a virtual environment
- Knowledge sharing for team members
- Positive outlook
- Proper, regular virtual training during the action learning process (to improve team strength and work quality)
- Regular meetings
- Using productivity tools to get feedback
- Using software or online tools for efficient task management and documentation.

Appendix III

Interview Excerpts from Action Learning Experts

This Appendix provides excerpts of interviews conducted in 2022 and 2023 with seasoned action learning professionals. They are presented below.

There are a total of thirteen topics on which we have gathered relevant content from the interviews, and they are organized under the following headers:

1. **The Definition of the Action Learning (AL) model used by Action Learning Associates, UK**
2. **Problem Statements in AL**
3. **How to Accelerate Action Learning (AAL)**
4. **Group Process/Issues and Challenges Concerning The Group/ Group Processes**
5. **Virtual Action Learning**
6. **Advantages/Benefits of AL/AAL**
7. **Reflection and Learning**
8. **Limitations (for example, culture, etc.) and Issues in AL**
9. **Uses of AL**
10. **Under What Circumstances AL Can Fail**
11. **Evaluation of AL**
12. **When Is AAL Appropriate**
13. **Similarities Between the Two Models (That of Action Learning Associates and the One Presented in this book)**

1. **The Definition of the Action Learning (AL) Model Used by Action Learning Associates**

   "A problem-solving reflective process where through questioning participants can access their inner knowledge and wisdom, to let that wisdom surface, to act in a way that they otherwise would not have done without the support of others. It is a reflective process."

   —**Jackie Draper,** *Senior Associate of Action Learning Associates. She has nearly 50 years of experience in AL.*

   "In the UK, the traditional approach to action learning involves creating space, with a small group of peers, for a person to think through a challenge they are facing. Participants pose questions to help that person grow in insight and find or create their own solutions."

   —**Nick Wright,** *Director, Action Learning Associates, UK.*

2. **Problem Statement in AL**

   "In an offsite location, senior leaders consisting of the CEO, the HR head, the business head, the CFO, the operating officers, and the employees, just one layer below them in the hierarchy, may be brought together to define the problem, understand what is happening."

   —**Dr. Mukul Joshi,** *Organization Development Facilitator, Leadership Coach, and Business Consultant.*

   "In an organization where I worked earlier, we identified what the employees were sad, mad, and glad about. The problem statement was constructed based on that aspect of the organization that gave employees sad and mad (angry) feelings."

   —**Abhishek Kumar,** *Head of HR, Lucknow International Airport Ltd.*

   "Participants focus on issues that are real and important for them, that they are finding complex and difficult to resolve, and where they have at least some opportunity to exercise personal agency and influence change."

   —**Nick Wright,** *Director, Action Learning Associates, UK.*

"The psychology of the members is such that, once they have identified a problem, they own it and work more willingly, unlike when told to address it."

—Abhishek Kumar, *Head of HR, Lucknow International Airport Ltd.*

3. **How to Accelerate Action Learning (AAL)**

Jane quotes Nancy Kline, author of *Time to Think,* that "the quality of everything we do depends first on the quality of our thinking." "If you go into organizations where they're so busy they don't have time to think, they're not likely to deliver good outcomes. Action learning provides people with space and time to think. I have facilitated action learning tasters for people, such as a breakfast taster, where I spend 20 minutes talking about action learning, and then the participants try it out. One can accelerate into the *doing* because that's where and how people learn. Action learning is a learning-by-doing methodology. Another way the learning can be supported is by asking the set members in the last session of the program to stay in touch with each other. If they then have a challenge or problem, they can email their set members and invite people to send their best questions to them. It could be a way for people to speedily get questions back by email that they could then think about and devise an action plan from having considered these questions. I think this can also be a way to accelerate the learning."

—Jane Garnham, *Facilitator, Coach, and Senior Associate with Action Learning Associates, UK*

"Timeboxing also becomes another critical thing because, when reflections happen, the reflections are not just at an intellectual level but also at an affective level. When affection comes in, the affective element comes in, the values and the needs that are spoken about and not spoken about, the unspeakable, start emerging, and that's where a facilitator faces the challenge. Here, s/he is concerned about holding the processes and the boundaries and using time wisely."

—Dr. Mukul Joshi, *Organization Development Facilitator, Leadership Coach, and Business Consultant.*

"The rigor and the nature of facilitation can accelerate the action learning process. The boundaries determined and the rigor will impact the speed."

—Jackie Draper, *Senior Associate of Action Learning Associates. She has close to 50 years of experience in AL.*

4. **Group Process/Issues and Challenges Concerning the Group/ Group Processes**

"On occasion, if a person gets completely stuck, perhaps because they have insufficient experience to find or create a way forward for themselves, we may offer an approach called 'peer-consultancy'. This involves a brief pause in the action learning process, where peers say tentatively what they *might* consider or do if they were in that person's situation, whilst the person simply listens. Importantly, the person is under no compulsion to respond to or act on any of those ideas."

—Nick Wright, *Director, Action Learning Associates, UK.*

"If there is less focus on the individual's development, when the facilitator focuses on the group process, the members will likely feel dismayed or not get their sense of return. This is where the facilitator's role becomes crucial."

—Dr. Mukul Joshi, *Organization Development Facilitator, Leadership Coach, and Business Consultant.*

"Action learning usually works best when the set members have a similar level of responsibility and authority."

—Mandy Hetherton, *Senior Associate, Action Learning Associates, UK.*

5. **Virtual Action Learning**

"In my experience, virtual action learning (VAL) can be very effective. One of the benefits is that it can make it possible to bring together people from different geographical locations or parts of the world by removing the barriers of travel time and travel costs. It can also enable us to bring people from different cultures and contexts, and thereby potentially holding very different perspectives, into a virtual room simultaneously."

—**Nick Wright,** *Director, Action Learning Associates, UK.*

"Blended programs work well (virtual and in-person). I have found that introverts often say they prefer online/virtual meetings."

—**Jane Garnham,** *Facilitator, Coach, and Senior Associate with Action Learning Associates, UK*

"In online mode, there are only two-dimensional data available. The third dimension is not available. So, it is a lot more intuition-based, the online work, rather than the data available three-dimensionally. Also, in some places/countries, connectivity is an issue, bandwidth is an issue, and the size of the meeting space is an issue; not everyone may have a marked or uninterrupted space. If one is interrupted and the video is switched off, the data will likely vanish; the continuity is disrupted. So, for action learning to work online, it requires a more rigorous commitment from the learner's point of view. It is also not that I (the learner) am not willing. I may be willing, but I may not have the opportunity. So, that is a challenge."

—**Dr. Mukul Joshi,** *Organization Development Facilitator, Leadership Coach, and Business Consultant.*

"With places where reach and internet connectivity are minor issues, practitioners have a different point of view."

—**Jackie Draper,** *Senior Associate, Action Learning Associates,* **says, "It works well but requires a specific skill set."**

6. **Advantages/Benefits of AL/AAL**

"I think, today, most information is available, so it is not like what I know isn't available to others. Everybody is likely to know. So, how does one apply what is available, and known, and which is scrutinized positively and not negatively for one to learn more effectively? It is through peer learning in AL. So, peer learning is one of the biggest advantages in AAL."

—**Dr. Mukul Joshi,** *Organization Development Facilitator, Leadership Coach, and Business Consultant.*

"Action learning is grounded in the concept of 'agency' (for more information, refer to: https://www.nick-wright.com/agents-of-change.html). When faced with complex challenges, people often feel bewildered, stuck, or powerless to influence change and move things forward. Action learning enables people to test their assumptions, expand the range of choices available, and get a greater sense of traction. In that sense, action learning is both empowering for individuals and transformational in the context in which they are working."

—**Nick Wright,** *Director Action Learning Associates, UK.*

"The skills, or let me call them life skills, that are developed during the actual learning process are transferable to any other aspect of life."

—**Jane Garnham,** *Facilitator, Coach, and Senior Associate with Action Learning Associates, UK*

"Set members toward the end say, "I manage my teams better now. Instead of giving them the answer, I now ask them the question." And then it's making them much more capable of resolving their problems."

—**Mandy Hetherton,** *Senior Associate, Action Learning Associates, UK.*

"Action learning generally works best if people have a choice about taking part because having somebody in a group who doesn't want to be there could have a very chilling or negative effect on the rest of the group."

—**Mandy Hetherton,** *Senior Associate, Action Learning Associates, UK.*

"The participants return as ones who can empower their staff. They learn to operate in ambiguity. They learn that there is not just one way and not just one single answer. They also realize that they are working in complexity and that there is no single answer or the best way to do things. They learn this through their peer experiences and reflection."

—**Jackie Draper,** *Senior Associate,*
Action Learning Associates, UK.

7. **Reflection and Learning**

"Reflection techniques, like 'river of life,' meditation, breathing technique, yoga, are used for reflection."

—**Dr. Mukul Joshi,** *Organization Development Facilitator,*
Leadership Coach, and Business Consultant.

"Instruments like DSQ40 (Defense Style Questionnaire) could also be used."

—**Abhishek Kumar,** *Head of HR, Lucknow*
International Airport Ltd.

"Reflection is the heart of action learning. It enables people to learn by thinking through issues deeply, discover insights by hearing diverse peers think through their issues differently, and practice skills, such as active listening, powerful questions, and team group work, that can be transfered into a wide range of roles and contexts."

—**Nick Wright,** *Director, Action Learning Associates, UK.*

"I invite the set members to maintain learning logs for reflection. I generally give them a template log or form and ask them to fill it in after a set meeting. I then encourage them to get the log out before we meet again and to think about what they have learned at the last session and how they have applied the learning. This process can help support and embed a reflective practice."

—**Jane Garnham,** *Facilitator, Coach, and Senior*
Associate with Action Learning Associates, UK

"I generally use the following questions to help the set members reflect, 'What has gone well?' 'What can we do differently to make it even better?' I might also say, reflect on yourself within this action learning set: 'How are you doing?' 'How are you showing up?' 'How sincerely do you think you're trying to work within the process?' 'How are you doing with the skills that you're developing?' 'What could you do to help yourself improve at asking questions or listening with your full attention?' So reflection is really at the heart of it. And then there are those mini invisible moments of reflection, where, if somebody is presenting an issue, they're reflecting on what they will share about it. They're remembering every time they've been asked a question. They're listening to what the person sharing their issue is saying. And they're reflecting; they're thinking, 'What am I hearing?' 'What might be helpful questions?' 'What's next?' So, it's intrinsic. There's hardly a moment in action learning without an opportunity to reflect."

—Mandy Hetherton, Senior Associate,
Action Learning Associates, UK.

"Once reflection deepens, people's learning deepens, and people tend to take that learning into many other settings, not just the set."

—Jackie Draper, Senior Associate,
Action Learning Associates, UK.

"At the end of each presentation, the facilitator would ask questions like, 'How have you worked together?' 'What have you noticed about the way we were working?' 'What questions enable you to deepen your thinking?' And then, at the end of the whole set, the set members would be asked, 'How are we developing as a set?' 'What has changed from last time?'"

—Jackie Draper, Senior Associate,
Action Learning Associates, UK.

"Everybody provides feedback to everybody. This is where the learning comes from."

—Jackie Draper, Senior Associate,
Action Learning Associates, UK.

8. **Limitations (For Example, Culture, etc.) and Issues in AL**

"Trust is a critical foundation for action learning sets. Reg Revans, the founder of Action Learning, invited participants to 'Swap your difficulties, not your cleverness.' This can feel counter-cultural for peers in, say, management of professional roles, who were often looked to and expected to provide answers for others. Action learning entails a willingness to make oneself vulnerable. In my experience, trust in a set grows when participants take risks and find themselves supported."

"In order to build trust, we focus on relationship building, that enables participants to know and understand each other, and con-tradicting ground rules that determine the set's culture and enable psychological safety. Creating specific opportunities for relationship building, e.g., via in-depth introductions and check-ins, is espe-cially important when working with virtual sets. Typical ground rules will include confidentiality, commitment contribution, curios-ity, and courage.

The benefits of action learning are amplified by diversity in a set. This is because it provides an opportunity for peers to post ques-tions from different perspectives and experience bases. It enables group participants to grow in awareness of their own assumptions, biases, and self-imposed or culturally imposed limits. I would always recommend maximum peer diversity, plus minimum hierar-chical-differential, to avoid the power dynamics that differences in such authority can create."

—Nick Wright, *Director, Action Learning Associates, UK.*

9. **Uses of AL**

"I have used action learning in leadership development and change management programmes. I've used action learning for newly qualified nurses in health trusts in the UK for the past six years and can evidence a positive impact story. I have also used action learning with mental health organizations. I worked with a local

Mind organization, and we offered action learning to people who were accessing their employment support programs. People found the process helpful and one individual described action learning, as "It has helped me do better at living."

—**Jane Garnham,** *Facilitator, Coach, and Senior Associate with Action Learning Associates, UK*

"I have used AL with National Health Service Trusts, in social care settings, such as care homes, with international organizations such as UNAIDS, and with many corporate organizations."

—**Mandy Hetherton,** *Senior Associate, Action Learning Associates, UK.*

10. **Under What Circumstances AL Can Fail**

"AL may fail to have a significant positive impact when it lacks internal sponsorship, and there has been an absence of an internal organizational culture of learning and reflection. This means there can be a contradiction between the culture inside the set and the wider cultural context. Also, if the 'busyness' of an organization means that it is hard to release six to seven people once every four to eight weeks for two to three hours, this organization may not be best suited to adopting action learning. That said, an action learning set program can sow seeds that may take root weeks, months, or years down the line."

—**Jane Garnham,** *Facilitator, Coach, and Senior Associate with Action Learning Associates, UK.*

11. **Evaluation of AL**

"The set members decide on a development objective at the beginning of the sessions and are asked to self-evaluate toward the end."

—**Jane Garnham,** *Facilitator, Coach, and Senior Associate with Action Learning Associates, UK*

"It's quite unusual to have any long-term evaluation; most evaluation is based on participant responses at the end of the action learning program."

—**Mandy Hetherton,** *Senior Associate,*
Action Learning Associates, UK.

12. **When is AAL appropriate?**

"If people already have listening and questioning skills, then I think you can help them become an independently functioning group sooner. And within a meeting, you might be able to do action learning a bit faster if the group is already skilled. But I would also say that I think part of what action learning offers that's important is a chance to slow down and pause and actually have some time to reflect. If we try to hurry that up, we risk losing something important. So, I will often warn people that, at the beginning, they might feel very impatient. I like to use the phrase: 'Go slow to get there faster.'"

—**Mandy Hetherton,** *Senior Associate,*
Action Learning Associates, UK.

13. **Similarities Between the Two Models (That of Action Learning Associates and the One Presented in This Book)**

"Both the UK and our model have reflection ingrained in them. Without this, learning is not possible. One of the major purposes of action learning is reflective practice and not just solving a problem."

—**Jackie Draper,** *Senior Associate,*
Action Learning Associates, UK.

Appendix IV

An Accelerated Action Learning Tabletop Role Play

Simulation

Overview

This tabletop role-play simulation is intended to allow managers and workers to experience a simulation of accelerated action learning in a day or less.

Objectives

Upon completing this simulation, participants can:

- Define what a tabletop role-play simulation is
- Describe how to conduct a tabletop role-play simulation
- Summarize the Accelerated Action Learning Model (AALM)
- Role-play each step of the AALM and debrief about it.

What is a Tabletop Role-Play?

A tabletop role-play has a long and venerable history. The best-known example of tabletop role-play is *Dungeons and Dragons*. In such a role-play, a case situation is described. Then participants in the role play are invited to select a character to play in a role play. The role-play facilitator plays the referee.

How Do You Play the Tabletop Role-Play Game?

The tabletop role-play game in this Appendix is a case study written to track—that is, align with—the steps in the Accelerated Action Learning Model (AALM). In each step, participants should:

- Read each case study vignette in each step of the AALM model
- Form small groups and spend about 15 minutes answering the questions following the case
- Return to the large group and debrief the answers to the questions
- Form small groups and spend about 20–30 minutes enacting a role play of the case vignette
- Return to the large group and debrief what happened in the role-play breakout groups
- Finish each step with an open discussion to reflect on what was learned in the step.

The facilitator for the session can vary these steps or drop steps.

A Note About Terms

- *The team leader* is a member of the AAL team and is a project manager. He or she monitors the team for business results.
- *The team facilitator* is a member of the AAL team, who influences others to ensure they learn individually and from each other.
- *The group facilitator* is the professor, trainer, or instructor overseeing the tabletop role-play experience. He or she is empowered to change any instructions and can change the time allowed for answering questions, debriefing questions and role play, and carrying out role plays.

Timing

While the group facilitator can change the timing for each step in the table-top role-play simulation, he or she will generally allow ten or more minutes for breakout teams to answer questions about the case vignette and about 20–30 minutes for breakout teams to role-play the case study vignette. Debriefs will typically take about five to ten minutes. Each step in the table-top role-play simulation should take at least 37 minutes. All ten steps will take at least 370 minutes, about six hours.

How Is Accelerated Action Learning Different from Traditional Action Learning?

Accelerated action learning differs from its traditional counterpart in several ways.

First, traditional action learning usually involves a team assembled to attack and solve a real business problem. It encourages cross-functional and occasionally cross-cultural teams. A major goal is to move employee development from formal settings, like classrooms or online programs, into "real-world settings." Workers learn simultaneously as they work to solve a business problem. The employer benefits by getting more results with the same work. Equal emphasis is placed on solving business problems and developing workers to think creatively and prepare for significant challenges.

In accelerated action learning, learners are encouraged to "speed up" their experimentation to find solutions to authentic (not staged) business problems or discover innovative approaches to address business issues. The logic is comparable to "rapid prototyping," in which the idea is to speed up learning, planning for failure but also planning to learn from fast failure.

In accelerated action learning, microlearning—which is understood to mean "learning in small chunks"—is embedded in every step of the AALM. That is unlike the traditional action learning model, in which workers on the action learning team may rely on a team facilitator to give them information or coach them on ways to attach problems.

The Accelerated Action Learning Model

The Accelerated Action Learning Model (AALM) follows these phases:

- *Phase 1*: Select a business problem, training challenge, organizational vision, or business goal
- *Phase 2*: Form a small group or team of people: each brings a skill, and each team member needs to build skills
- *Phase 3*: Brief the team members
- *Phase 4*: Establish measurable goals for the accelerated action learning set
- *Phase 5*: Encourage team members to experiment with solutions
- *Phase 6*: Place equal emphasis on business results and individual development
- *Phase 7*: Complete the accelerated action learning set

- *Phase 8*: Debrief the accelerated action learning team members collectively
- *Phase 9*: Debrief the accelerated action learning team members individually
- *Phase 10*: Reassign accelerated action learning team members on their individual development needs.

How Is This Tabletop Role-Play Simulation Organized?

This tabletop role-play simulation is organized around the phases of the accelerated action learning model. For each step, participants should:

- Read the case vignette for each step
- Break out into teams and answer the questions at the end of each case vignette
- Return to the larger group and debrief the answers to the questions appearing after the case vignette
- Break out into teams and role-play the case study vignette
- Return to the larger group and debrief what happened in the role-play groups
- Hold an open discussion to reflect on what was learned about action learning in this vignette.

The Case Situation

The Amalgamated Manufacturing Company, hereinafter abbreviated to Amalgamated, manufactures spray cans. Amalgamated is often placed on contract by other companies to fill hairspray cans, deodorant cans, and other personal care products. (The company does not accept contracts for other spray products—such as insect sprays.) The company consists of one industrial plant with five hundred workers. The company has a production department with four hundred workers; a financial division with twenty workers; a human resources division with ten workers; a marketing department with thirty-five workers; and an IT (computer) department with thirty-five workers. The company is 50 years old and operates in a small town of 11,000 people in the US Midwest. In recent years, the company has varied its workforce, laying people off briefly when sales are down and hiring when sales are up.

The quick summary in the next section summarizes all characters in the case vignettes.

The CEO of Amalgamated has decided that the company needs to do a better job of unleashing the natural creative thinking of its workers. He wants to experiment with accelerated action learning (AAL).

Quick Summary of the Characters

Key characters in this tabletop role play include:

- *John Krishna* is the CEO. He is 39 years old and has been the CEO for five years. He is energetic.
- *Laura Kolb* is VP of HR. She is twenty-eight and very personable.
- *Benny Bengsten* is VP of Production. He is 58 years old and has been a Production Manager for 30 years at Amalgamated.
- *Fanny Brice* is VP of Marketing.
- *Larry Grunderson* is VP of IT.
- *Morton Wile* is the Chief Financial Officer (CFO).
- *Gordon Lawson* is an accountant in the financial division.
- *Robert Benson* is President of the company's union.
- *Harry S. Smith* is a high-potential middle manager who reports to Fanny Brice. He is forty-two.
- *Brianna Olsen* is a front-line supervisor in the production department.
- *Penny Babb* is a front-line programmer in the IT department.
- *Aleisha Twain* is a front-line worker in the production department.
- *Marsha Magginson* is a supervisor in the marketing division. She is the team leader.
- *Mary Marina* is a middle manager in human resources. She is the team facilitator.
- *Harold Gunderson* is the manager of the spray can assembly line.

When participants select their parts, they may give their characters any traits or attributes they wish. Participants may reflect their feelings as "difficult to work with," "a wonderful worker," or any other personality traits they would like to use.

Note that, in this Tabletop Role Play, it is assumed you will have a trainer, a group facilitator, or a professor to organize each step and to offer specific instructions on how to divide up into breakout groups, how much time to allow, and any special instructions that the trainer, group facilitator or professor will offer for any steps. In the instructions below, this role is called the *group facilitator*. That term refers to the trainer, instructor, or professor.

The Steps in the Tabletop Role Play

Step 1: Select A Business Problem, Training Challenge, Organizational Vision, or Business Goal

Case Vignette. *Benny Bengsten* wants to try accelerated action learning. He also felt that, by doing so, he would set an example that would encourage workers to self-organize as they noticed problems in the organization.

One assembly line in the plant has problems on its night shift, operating from 11 p.m. to 7 a.m. (The plant runs 24 hours a day, seven days a week, 365 days a year.) Benny formed an AAL team to investigate the problem and explore practical solutions. Benny wanted to talk to some people about it first. So, he called his manager Harry Gunderson into his office to discuss AAL and to describe why he wanted to use it.

Questions about the Case Vignette. *Form breakout groups of seven to nine people and devote a few minutes—the exact time will be provided by your group facilitator, trainer, or professor—to answer the questions.*

1. *Under what conditions is it appropriate to form an AAL team?*
2. *Under what conditions is it inappropriate to form an AAL team?*
3. *Who determines when an AAL team should be formed?*

Debrief the Questions about the Case. *The group facilitator should ask for answers to the questions from different teams.*

The Role Play. *Form breakout groups of seven to nine people and devote 20–30 minutes—the exact time will be decided by your group facilitator, trainer, or professor—to role-play the case vignette. Two people should pick their parts. One person should play Gunderson, and one person should play Benny. Act out the discussion. Other participants should play observers and prepare to debrief after completing the role play.*

Debrief of the Role Play. *The group facilitator should ask observers to discuss what happened in the role plays they observed.*

Open Discussion of Reflections. *What do you think was revealed from the role play? What did you learn from it?*

Step 2: Form a Small Group or Team of People, Who Each Brings a Skill, and Has a Need to Build Skills

Case Vignette*.* Bengsten wanted to build bridges across the organization as part of that effort. He asked other departments if they would volunteer workers to participate on an AAL team. Benny assembled a team of workers that included:

- *A*, a front-line programmer in the IT department.
- *B*, a front-line worker in the production department.
- *C*, a supervisor in the marketing division. She has been appointed team leader, meaning she is responsible for ensuring the team gets business results and complies with limitations on the time, money, and other limitations on team performance.
- *D*, an accountant in the financial division.
- *E*, a middle manager in human resources. She has been appointed team facilitator, meaning she is responsible for ensuring that team members meet their individual development goals, while on the team, and learn from each other.
- *F*, the manager of the spray can assembly line.

Bengsten realized the workers could not be assigned to the project full-time. He assembled them and limited their time to half a day per week. He received approval from the managers of these workers to participate. He ensured that participation on the AAL team was listed as part of the key performance indicators (KPIs) for their annual performance reviews.

Questions about the Case Vignette*. Form breakout groups of seven to nine people and devote a few minutes—the exact time will be provided by your group facilitator, trainer, or professor—to answer the questions.*

1. *How much should the CEO support AAL before it is used?*
2. *Who are the decision-makers whose support is critical for AAL to work, in your team's opinion? Why do you believe so?*

Debrief of the Questions about the Case*. The group facilitator should ask for answers to the questions from different teams.*

The Role Play*. Form breakout groups of seven to nine people and devote 20–30 minutes—the exact time will be decided by your group facilitator,* *trainer, or professor—to role-play the case vignette. Members of each breakout time should pick their parts. One person should play each part listed below:*

- *A*, a front-line programmer in the IT department.
- *B*, a front-line worker in the production department.
- *C*, a supervisor in the marketing division. She is the team leader.
- *D*, an accountant in the financial division.
- *E*, a middle manager in human resources. She is the team facilitator.
- *F*, the manager of the spray can assembly line.

If the gender balance on the breakout team does not match the characters, then a male can play a female character, or a female can play a male character. One person should play Benny Bengsten.

In this role play, the breakout team should act out the case study and discuss who is on the team, what skills they bring, and what skills they need to learn to be developed for more responsibility or more challenging technical roles in the organization.

Debrief of the Role Play. *The group facilitator should ask observers to discuss what happened in the role plays they observed.*

Open Discussion of Reflections. *What do you think was revealed from the role play? What did you learn from it?*

Step 3: Brief the Team Members

Case Vignette. *Benny Bengsten met with the team members to tell them about the problems on the night shift. He will share the high rejection rate of products made on the night shift and give them whatever other information he has about the situation. But he will also tell the team he lacks complete information and that part of their job on the AAL team is to investigate the problem(s) and the solution(s).*

Recall that the team members are:

- *A*, a front-line programmer in the IT department.
- *B*, a front-line worker in the production department.
- *C*, a supervisor in the marketing division. She has been appointed team leader, meaning she is responsible for ensuring the team gets business results and complies with limitations on the time, money, and other limitations on team performance.
- *D*, an accountant in the financial division.

- *E*, a middle manager in human resources. She has been appointed team facilitator, meaning she is responsible for ensuring that team members meet their individual development goals, while on the team, and learn from each other.
- *F*, the manager of the spray can assembly line.

Questions about the Case Vignette*. Form breakout groups of seven to nine people and devote a few minutes—the exact time will be provided by your group facilitator, trainer, or professor—to answer the questions.*

1. *Why is it necessary for Benny to inform the team that "he lacks complete information and that part of their job on the AAL team is to investigate the problem(s) as well as the solution(s)?"*
2. *Why does the decision-maker have to brief the team? Could there be occasions when the team should not wait for a decision-maker briefing and "jump in on their own and find out what is happening?"*

Debrief of the Questions about the Case*. The group facilitator should ask for answers to the questions from different teams.*

   The Role Play*. Form breakout groups of seven to nine people and devote 20–30 minutes—the exact time will be decided by your group facilitator, trainer, or professor—to role-play the case vignette. One person should play Benny Bengsten. Other people should play the members of the team, which includes:*

- *A*, a front-line programmer in the IT department.
- *B*, a front-line worker in the production department.
- *C*, a supervisor in the marketing division. She is the team leader.
- *D*, an accountant in the financial division.
- *E*, a middle manager in human resources. She is the team facilitator.
- *F*, the manager of the spray can assembly line.

If additional members are on the team, besides Bengsten, Babb, Twain, Magginson, Lawson, Marina, and Gunderson, those members should play the role of observers and watch what happens during the role play. During the role play, the team should act out what happened in the case study vignette, demonstrating what it is like to brief an AAL team.

   Debrief of the Role Play*. The group facilitator should ask observers to discuss what happened in the role plays they observed.*

Open Discussion of Reflections. *What do you think was revealed from the role play? What did you learn from it?*

Step 4: Establish Measurable Goals for the Accelerated Action Learning Set

Case Vignette. *As Benny Bengsten briefs the team about the problem, he realizes that he needs to give the team some way to assess their efforts as they experiment with possible solutions to the quality problems affecting the assembly line on the night shift. Benny notes that the rejection rate for products (spray cans) on the night shift is double that of the normal shifts. Although Benny would love for the shift's rejection rate to match that of other shifts, he realizes that may not happen. He sets the measurable goal for the AAL set to reduce the rejection rate to 80 percent of the average rejection rate for all other shifts.*

Questions about the Case Vignette. *Form breakout groups of seven to nine people and devote a few minutes—the exact time will be provided by your group facilitator, trainer, or professor—to answer the questions.*

1. *How should an AAL team's measurable goals be established? Should the decision-maker always do that, or are there other ways to establish measurable goals?*
2. *Why should the goals be measurable? What are the risks if they are not made measurable?*

Debrief of the Questions about the Case. *The group facilitator should ask for answers to the questions from different teams.*

The Role Play. *Form breakout groups of seven to nine people and devote 20–30 minutes—the exact time will be decided by your group facilitator, trainer, or professor—to role-play the case vignette. One person should play Benny Bengsten. Other people should play these parts:*

- *A,* a front-line programmer in the IT department.
- *B,* a front-line worker in the production department.
- *C,* a supervisor in the marketing division. She is the team leader.
- *D,* an accountant in the financial division.
- *E,* a middle manager in human resources. She is the team facilitator.
- *F,* manager of the spray can assembly line.

*If the gender balance on the breakout team does not match the charac-
ters, then a male can play a female character, or a female can play a male
character.*

*In this role play, Bengsten sets measurable targets for the team. That hap-
pens during the team briefing. Team members may question him about his
measurable target.*

Debrief of the Role Play. *The group facilitator should ask for observers
to discuss what happened in the role plays they observed.*

Open Discussion of Reflections. *What do you think was revealed from
the role play? What did you learn from it?*

Step 5: Encourage Team Members to Experiment with Solutions

Case Vignette. *This step is the heart of accelerated action learning. The
team members should experiment with many solutions quickly to reduce the
quality control problems on the assembly line. In this case vignette, assume
that the quality control problem's root causes have been identified as follows: (1) during the night shift, workers are sleepy and sometimes fall asleep;
(2) machine operators complain that there are many problems with obsolete
equipment on the assembly line, and (3) company management rarely vis-
its the assembly line with quality problems. The team members listed below
should discuss ways to address the root causes to solve all three problems.
In this case vignette, they will also list ways to use microlearning to explore
methods to solve the problems by addressing the root causes.*

Questions about the Case Vignette. *Form breakout groups of seven
to nine people and devote a few minutes—the exact time will be decided
by your group facilitator, trainer, or professor—to answer the following
questions:*

1. *What role should the team leader play in experimenting with solutions?*
2. *What role should the team facilitator play in experimenting with
   solutions?*
3. *What role should team members play in experimenting with solutions?*
4. *What is microlearning, and how can it be used to discover and experiment with possible solutions? List types of microlearning and how they
   can be applied to AAL.*
5. *How can the team members speed up the experimentation process?*

Debrief of the Questions about the Case. *The group facilitator should ask
for answers to the questions from different teams.*

The Role Play. *Form breakout groups of seven to nine people and devote 20–30 minutes—the exact time will be decided by your group facilitator, trainer, or professor—to role-play the case vignette. Team members should select their parts. Be sure that one person plays Marsha Magginson, the team leader, and one person plays Marsha Marina, the team facilitator. Other team members may include:*

- *A, a front-line programmer in the IT department.*
- *B, a front-line worker in the production department.*
- *D, an accountant in the financial division.*
- *F, the manager of the spray can assembly line.*

If over nine people participate in the session, then the additional participants should adopt the roles of team observers. If there are no team observers, any team member can play that role.

Debrief of the Role Play. *The group facilitator should ask for observers to discuss what happened in the role plays they observed.*

Open Discussion of Reflections. *What do you think was revealed from the role play? What did you learn from it?*

Step 6: Place Equal Emphasis on Business Results and Individual Development

Case Vignette. *The team members set up experiments—because engineers use the term "experiment"—and explore different solutions. As they do so, the team leader focuses on how their efforts contribute to business results, and the team facilitator focuses on the team members and how their efforts contribute to developing the skills of each team member. One way this is done is through weekly team meetings in which experiments are implemented, and then the team leader hosts a discussion of the results. Then, the team facilitator hosts a discussion of what team members learned individually and collectively.*

Questions about the Case Vignette. *Form breakout groups of seven to nine people and devote a few minutes—the exact time will be decided by your group facilitator, trainer, or professor—to answer these questions:*

1. *How can a team leader focus on business results during an AAL set?*
2. *How can a team facilitator focus attention on the individual development of team members?*

3. *How could a team facilitator focus attention on developing the team members collectively?*
4. *How can microlearning be applied to focus attention on business results?*
5. *How can microlearning be applied to focusing attention on individual skill development?*

Debrief on the Questions about the Case. *The group facilitator should ask for answers to the questions from different teams.*

The Role Play. *Form breakout groups of seven to nine people and devote 20–30 minutes—the exact time will be decided by your group facilitator, trainer, or professor—to role-play the case vignette. The participants in the breakout groups should pick their parts and assume whatever description of the character they portray as they wish. This role play should focus on how a team leader hosts a discussion of team results and how a team facilitator hosts a discussion of individual and collective learning. Remember that the team members are:*

- *A, a front-line programmer in the IT department.*
- *B, a front-line worker in the production department.*
- *D, an accountant in the financial division.*
- *F, the manager of the spray can assembly line.*

Debrief of the Role Play. *The group facilitator should ask for observers to discuss what happened in the role plays they observed.*

Open Discussion of Reflections. *What do you think was revealed from the role play? What did you learn from it?*

Step 7: Complete the Accelerated Action Learning Set

Case Vignette. *At some point, the AAL team will reach a limitation set at the outset of the accelerated action learning set. Examples of limitations include constraints on time (how long to spend on experimenting with possible solutions), money (how much of a budget, if any budget, the AAL team has been given), staffing (how much freedom does the AAL team have to draw on help from outside the team during their experiments), and solutions (how much measurable results should experiments achieve to be deemed successful or unsuccessful). But it is clear that the team will reach a limitation at some point. The AAL set should stop. In this case, what should happen? The team* *solved the quality control problem of the night shift. But now they must cease their efforts and present them to Benny Bengsten.*

Questions about the Case Vignette. *Form breakout groups of seven to nine people and devote a few minutes—the exact time will be decided by your group facilitator, trainer, or professor—to answer these questions:*

1. *What should be done if an AAL team fails to solve the problem they were tasked to solve?*
2. *Could there ever be occasions when an AAL team simply "gives up"? What should the team leader and/or team facilitator do then?*
3. *Could there be occasions when an AAL team wishes to give up, but the manager sponsoring the AAL team demands that they continue to experiment? What is likely to happen in situations like that?*

Debrief of the Questions about the Case. *The group facilitator should ask for answers to the questions from different teams.*

The Role Play. *Form breakout groups of seven to nine people and devote 20–30 minutes—the exact time will be provided by your group facilitator, trainer, or professor—to role-play the case vignette. In this role play, team members should select their parts (roles) and act out how to brief their sponsor Barry Bengsten on what results they got from their efforts. Assume that the group produced effective solutions to the case vignette problem and slashed the reject rate of the night shift assembly line.*

Recall that the team members include:

- *A*, a front-line programmer in the IT department.
- *B*, a front-line worker in the production department.
- *C*, a supervisor in the marketing division. She has been appointed team leader, meaning she is responsible for ensuring the team gets business results and complies with limitations on the time, money, and other resources on team performance.
- *D*, an accountant in the financial division.
- *E*, a middle manager in human resources. She has been appointed team facilitator, meaning she is responsible for ensuring that team members meet their individual development goals while on the team and learn from each other.
- *F*, manager of the spray can assembly line.

Debrief of the Role Play. *The group facilitator should ask for observers to discuss what happened in the role plays they observed.*

Open Discussion of Reflections. *What do you think was revealed from the role play? What did you learn from it?*

Step 8: Debrief the Accelerated Action Learning Team Members Collectively

Case Vignette. *Once the AAL team sponsor—that is, Benny Bengsten—has accepted the AAL team solution, then the team facilitator should host a discussion about what the team members learned from the AAL experience. Since the team members were geographically dispersed, the team debrief of the AAL experience occurred by videoconference (Zoom).*

    Questions about the Case Vignette. *Form breakout groups of seven to nine people and devote a few minutes—the exact time will be decided by your group facilitator, trainer, or professor—to answer these questions:*

1. *What kind of questions should a team facilitator ask an AAL team to reveal team members' perceptions of what they learned as a group? List the questions.*
2. *What questions should a team leader ask an AAL team to reveal team members' perceptions of how well they worked together as a cohesive group to achieve business results?*
3. *How might a facilitated session over videoconference differ from a face-to-face one? Why might that difference be important in capturing team perceptions of what team members learned from the AAL experience?*

Debrief of the Questions about the Case. *The group facilitator should ask for answers to the questions from different teams.*

    The Role Play. *Form breakout groups of seven to nine people and devote 20–30 minutes—the exact time will be decided by your group facilitator, trainer, or professor—to role-play the case vignette. One person should play team leader, and one should play team facilitator. The team facilitator should role-play how to debrief an AAL team. Others should play team members during that debrief.*

    Recall that the team members are:

- *A*, a front-line programmer in the IT department.
- *B*, a front-line worker in the production department.
- *D*, an accountant in the financial division.
- *F*, manager of the spray can assembly line.

Debrief of the Role Play. The group facilitator should ask for observers to discuss what happened in the role plays they observed.

 Open Discussion of Reflections. What do you think was revealed from the role play? What did you learn from it?

Step 9: Debrief the Accelerated Action Learning Team Members Individually

Case Vignette. Accelerated action learning places equal emphasis on getting business results and developing team members. Although the group facilitator can debrief the AAL team about what the team members learned collectively, it is also wise to hold individual meetings with each team member to list out: (1) what each team member learned from the AAL experience; and (2) what skills each team member should learn—and perhaps through new AAL experiences. In this vignette, assume the team facilitator is discussing with ONE team member. Pick whichever team member you wish. One person plays team facilitator; one person plays one team member; other team members play the role of observers.

 Questions about the Case Vignette. Form breakout groups of seven to nine people and devote a few minutes—the exact time will be decided by your group facilitator, trainer, or professor– to answer these questions:

1. Where should such a meeting be held?
2. Why do you think the setting of a meeting makes a difference?

Debrief of the Questions about the Case. The group facilitator should ask for answers to the questions from different teams.

 The Role Play. Form breakout groups of seven to nine people and devote 20–30 minutes—the exact time will be decided by your group facilitator, trainer, or professor—to role-play the case vignette. One person should play the team facilitator. A second person should play any member of the team. All other team members in this role play should enact the role of observers.

 The full cast of characters is as follows:

- *A*, a front-line programmer in the IT department.
- *B*, a front-line worker in the production department.
- *C*, a supervisor in the marketing division. She has been appointed team leader, meaning she is responsible for ensuring the team gets business results and complies with limitations on the time, money, and other limitations on team performance.

- *D*, an accountant in the financial division.
- *E*, a middle manager in human resources. She has been appointed team facilitator, meaning she is responsible for ensuring that team members meet their individual development goals while on the team and learn from each other.
- *F*, manager of the spray can assembly line.

Debrief of the Role Play. *The group facilitator should ask for observers to discuss what happened in the role-play they observed.*

    Open Discussion of Reflections. *What do you think was revealed from the role play? What did you learn from it?*

Step 10: Reassign Accelerated Action Learning Team Members on Their Individual Development Needs

Case Vignette. *At the end of this AAL set, each team member has identified skills he or she needs to develop through future work experience and through future AAL experiences. In this case vignette, assume that Benny Bengsten meets with the team leader and team facilitator to discuss each team member and what he/she needs to learn to be developed further. The purpose of the meeting is to identify one or more AAL experiences that may be hosted by the company.*

    Questions about the Case Vignette. *Form breakout groups of seven to nine people and devote a few minutes—the exact time will be decided by your group facilitator, trainer, or professor—to answer these questions:*

1. *Many talent development specialists speak of the well-known 70-20-10 rule. Where does accelerated action learning fall in those 70-20-10 categories?*
2. *Accelerated action learning is not the only way to build competencies or skills— what are other ways? Under what conditions might AAL be a preferred way to develop skills or competencies?*
3. *When might AAL not be appropriate to build skills or competencies?*
4. *Could microlearning be used in deciding on who and how to reassign AAL team members? Explain why or why not.*

Debrief of the Questions about the Case. *The group facilitator should ask for answers to the questions from different teams.*

The Role Play*. Form breakout groups of seven to nine people and devote 20–30 minutes—the exact time will be decided by your group facilitator, trainer, or professor—to role-play the case vignette. One person should play Benny Bengsten, one person should play team leader Marsha Magginson, and one person should play team facilitator Mary Marina. Act out the role play. Other team members should play observers, watching what happens during the role play. Observers should be prepared to report on what they observed during the role play.*

Debrief of the Role Play*. The group facilitator should ask observers to discuss what happened in the role plays they observed.*

Open Discussion of Reflections*. What do you think was revealed from the role play? What did you learn from it?*

Appendix V

Selected Resources for Action Learning

What follows are resources to take you further in action learning.

Selected Books

Boshyk, Y., & Dilworth, R. (Eds.). (2010). *Action learning: History and evolution.* Palgrave.

O'Neil, J., & Marsick, V. (2007). *Understanding action learning.* Amacom.

Marquardt, M., Banks, S., Cauweiler, P., & Sengng, C. (2018). *Optimizing the power of action learning.* 3rd ed. Nicholas Brealey.

Revans, R. W. (2011). *ABC of action learning.* Gower Publishing Company.

Selected Articles

Cho, Y. (2013). What is action learning? Components, types, processes, issues, and research agendas. *Learning and Performance Quarterly, 1*(4), 1–11.

Rigg, C., & Trehan, K. (2004). Reflections on working with critical action learning. *Action Learning: Research and Practice, 1*(2), 151–167.

Zuber-Skerritt, O. (2002). The concept of action learning. *The Learning Organization, 9*(3), 114–124. https://doi.org/10.1108/09696470210428831

Selected Videos

Action Learning Centre. *What is action learning?* https://www.actionlearningcentre .com/about-action-learning

QAATubel. *Introducing action learning sets.* https://www.youtube.com/watch?v
=vLIcLeoq_Og

Smartsims. *On action learning by Frank Voehl.* https://www.smartsims.com/teach-
ing-methods/on-action-learning-by-frank-voehl/

Selected Associations on Action Learning

The Action Learning, Action Research Association Ltd. https://www.alarassociation
.org/

World Institute for Action Learning. https://wial.org/action-learning/library/

International Foundation for Action Learning. https://ifal.org.uk

Selecting Resources on Microlearning

Bacsich, P. (2012). The cost-and time-effectiveness of online learning: Providing a
perspective on microlearning and the difference between academic and corporate views. https://www.academia.edu/13029473/Time_and_e_learning_The
_cost_and_time_effectiveness_of_online_learning_providing_a_perspective
_on_Microlearning_and_the_differences_between_academic_and_corporate
_views

Corbeil, J., Khan, B., & Corbeil, M. (Eds.). (2021). *Microlearning in the digital age:
The design and delivery of learning in snippets.* Routledge.

Kapp, K., & Defelice, R. (2019). *Microlearning: Short and sweet.* Association for
Talent Development.

Riis, R. (2021). *What is microlearning?* https://www.youtube.com/watch?v
=KlbsuPAibfY

Time as a Strategic Resource

Suresh Kumar, P. M. & Aithal, S. (2020). Time as a strategic resource in management of organizations. MPRA Paper 104026, University Library of Munich,
Germany.

Action Learning Across Different Industries

Abbott, C., Jones, V. L., Sexton, M. G., & Lu, S. L. (2007). Action learning as an
enabler for successful technology transfer with construction SMEs. *RICS
Research Paper Series,* 7(16), 1–41.

Seddon, J., & Caulkin, S. (2007). Systems thinking, lean production and action learning. *Action Learning: Research and Practice, 4*(1), 9–24.

Reflection in Action Learning

Dilworth, R. L. (2005). *Creating opportunities for reflection in action learning.* ITAP International. https://link.springer.com/chapter/10.1057/9780230250734_1
Kelliher, F. (2014). Just do it: Action learning as a catalyst for reflective practice on an MBA programme. *Procedia-Social and Behavioral Sciences, 141,* 1275–1280.

Virtual Action Learning

Dickenson, M., Burgoyne, J., & Pedler, M. (2010). Virtual action learning: Practices and challenges. *Action Learning: Research and Practice, 7*(1), 59–72.
Nasongkhla, J., & Sujiva, S. (2022). A hyFlex-flipped class in action learning: A connectivist MOOC for creative problem-solving. *Contemporary Educational Technology, 14*(4), ep392.
Plack, M. M., Dunfee, H., Rindflesch, A., & Driscoll, M. (2008). Virtual action learning sets: A model for facilitating reflection in the clinical setting. *Journal of Physical Therapy Education, 22*(3), 33–42.

Facilitation in Action Learning

O'Neil, J. (1999). Facilitating action learning the role of the learning coach. *Advances in Developing Human Resources, 1*(2), 39–55.
Segal-Horn, S., McGill, I., Bourner, T., & Frost, P. (1987). Non-facilitated action learning. *Management Education and Development, 18*(4), 277–286.

Learning in Action Learning

Marquardt, M., & Waddill, D. (2004). The power of learning in action learning: A conceptual analysis of how the five schools of adult learning theories are incorporated within the practice of action learning. *Action Learning: Research and Practice, 1*(2), 185–202.

Index

Printed in the United States
by Baker & Taylor Publisher Services